PROGRESSIVE REVELATION

PROGRESSIVE REVELATION

God's Permanent Dialogue with Humanity

Reynaldo Pareja

To order additional copies of this book, contact:
Xlibris
1-888-795-4274
www.Xlibris.com
Orders@Xlibris.com
722056

CONTENTS

Acknowledgements... xi
Introduction xiii

Chapter 1 Basic Assumptions.................................1
   Man makes gods of nature's powers.........................2
   Man Evolves from Animism to the gods of Olympus 4
   The fundamental question about what happens
      after death 11
   Nature's innermost organization..............................14
   Man cannot know the Essence of God.....................16
   God 'must' reveal Himself.......................................18

Chapter 2 How Does God Reveal Himself?......................25
   Requirements of God's Spokesperson......................26
   Historical Evidence of These Messengers 28
   The Messenger Speaks in the Name of God 30

Chapter 3 How can God appear among us?.....................33
   God the Creator..33
   The Creative Word 38

Chapter 4 The Manifestation's Mission 52
   Summarizing the previous explanations....................52
   The Mission of all Manifestations 53
   The relationship of each Manifestation with His
      predecessor 55
   The uniqueness of the Revelation of each
      Manifestation..59
   Duration of the Manifestation's cycle.......................62

Chapter 5 Progressive Revelation................................67
   How to understand Progressive Revelation? 67

God directs the spiritual, intellectual, and even
    material evolution of man 70
Examples of Progressive Revelation 74
Worshipping the only one God 75
Burnt Offerings 76
How to Pray to God 78
Not to initiate war 81
No stealing 85
Matrimony 86
Dedicate one day to the Acknowledgement and
    Adoration of God, the Creator 90
Woman's equality to man 92

Chapter 6 Our Relationship to the Manifestation 103
Recognition 103
Trust and Certainty 104
Being Thankful for His Life/Revelation 106
Following the Manifestation 107
Proclaiming the new message 111
Service to Others, Service to the Cause of the
    Manifestation 113

Chapter 7 God's Plan 117
Role of a father 117
The Role of God 120
God's Plan 122
The Manifestation's divine force stimulates
    development 125

Chapter 8 The most recent Manifestation 131
Arrival of the New Manifestation 131
Affirmation of being God's Spokesperson 140
The return of all previous Messengers 142
The "golden measure" of the true Spokesperson
    of God 144
Bahá'u'lláh fulfills the prophesies of the second
    coming 145
Prophecies of Bahá'u'lláh that have been fulfilled 149

Chapter 9 The New Revelation 154
        The Báb 155
        Bahá'u'lláh 156
        Religious persecution and warfare 157
        Oneness of religion and of humanity 162
        Unity of Humanity 168

Conclusion 173
Bibliography 181

To all those who question if God is still present in our human history or if He has ceased talking to us after his Prophet, Mohammad.

Acknowledgements

A book that has something important to say is not the work of only one author. If the ideas expressed within can potentially impact its readers, whom the author will never have the opportunity to meet personally, it is necessary that the book be reviewed by enough friends, colleagues, and experts on the subject to get the best overall result. Only then can the author aspire to engage the reader in its content.

This book is not exempt from this interactive process because the very subject requires it. Therefore, I have the honor to thank many people because at some time during the process of writing, they gave their opinions, offered insights, proposed alternatives, suggested improvements.

Thus, I am pleased to mention those who helped with editing the Spanish text. Jose Luis Marques's keen insights helped me structure the book. Rodolfo de Roux, a dear friend, did a wonderful job of polishing grammar construction and thought clarity, and then my wife and life-long companion, Patricia Pareja, who always manages to find punctuation errors.

The quality of the Spanish version is also the product of several people whose generosity in reviewing the manuscript provided excellent comments, suggestions, observations, and modifications. In order of participation, I must mention Marilyn Smith, Rosemary Baily, Ronny Brennes, Jeff Miller, Ana Hilda Lemus, Fernando Herrera, Joe Coblentz, and Ted Breton.

This English version of the book also has a list of collaborators that must be mentioned since, without their help, it could have not been written. I would like to start the list with Tamara Benson (a long time high school colleague) who made the first draft translation into English. Then, several editors helped along the way with one or several chapters. I am thus indebted to Sue Benjamin who edited the bulk of the chapters with extraordinary insight into the content of the book, once more followed by Joe Coblentz. Others that contributed with edits of specific chapters were Marc Bogan, a long time friend that I had lost contact since university days, and Suzi Mickler, a pioneer resident in Belize.

Many thanks to each one of you. You made possible the birth of this reflection that we hope gives light and perspective to the unfathomable mystery of how God can communicate with us given the insurmountable chasm that exists between Him, the Creator, and us humans, the created.

Introduction

Some of the fundamental questions that millions have asked throughout mankind's history is "If God exists, who is He, how can I know Him, is it possible to imagine Him, how can I talk to Him? Is God another of our mental categories and, therefore product of our imagination, a figment of our brain chemistry, or does God really exist and has communicated with us in a verifiable and objective manner revealing to us who He really is?

Adjacent to these questions exists the inseparable doubt about our affirmations---is God one of our mental categories, a product of our fertile imagination, or does He has a reality of Being that we cannot grasp?

This questioning has led to many confrontations between those who believe that such communication has taken place and those who affirm that God has never spoken to us. The former assertion is based on our intuitive knowing that the billions of human beings living in this blue dot, Earth, were created by a power greater than natural evolution. This power is the origin of all that is, and is Self-subsisting, Eternal, and Creator. The latter assertion states that since there is no reliable, scientific evidence that God has communicated with us, He is thus, a product of our imagination.

It is, therefore, necessary to make a historical/critical and in-depth study to find out if there exists or if there is a possibility of communication between this being – God —and us, Humanity.

If communication has already occurred, then, in what manner has it happened? If it already occurred, what has God revealed about Himself that helps us understand who He is; what is His ultimate Essence?

If we find no indication that communication of God to man has transpired at any time during the history of Humanity, then we can conclude with some certainty that God is more our own mind's creation rather than a transcendental reality that has manifested and revealed Himself to us.

The time we spend on Earth is merely a brief moment during which we eagerly seek and ask, "What is the reason for and meaning of our Existence?" We hope that the book's reflection of this ever present question provides the reader with suggestions to arrive at a satisfactory answer, one that fills with optimism our daily pilgrimage until we attain the presence of our Creator.

Chapter 1

Basic Assumptions

The affirmation that god(s) exist – is it the product of a natural mental process that man has developed during his evolutionary journey on Earth? Or has God spoken to Humanity in an intelligible manner that we can understand who He is?

Before answering this question, the basis of this book, it is first necessary to clarify that there are two paths by which man can say or affirm something about God. The first is that man, as a thinking being, imaginative and creative par excellence, has constructed an image, an explanation; has created a concept, a definition of Who is God or who are the gods who exist in the transcendent no-space-time dimension that man cannot enter voluntarily. The second alternative to learn something correctly about Who God is would be that out of His own initiative and via the path He has chosen, God has communicated with man. In this communication God has revealed something about Himself in such a clear, understandable manner that man can form an idea, an image, a correct conception of Who He is.

Let's explore the first path; that is, let us investigate if man has attempted to define Who God is or who are those other gods he has affirmed exist. We should then ask if man has left behind any testimony, some documentation by which he has described how he perceived the existence of gods, and the way they have related with humans.

The answer is "Yes". We have ample documentation, left to us by entire civilizations that described the belief in the existence of these gods and the manner they related to man. Today we identify these descriptions and explanations as myths and mythology, archetypes conceived in order to explain the forces of nature (that man could not control) and the possible relationship that man had with them. Such myths and explanations are Mankind's collective effort to find answers to lifelong questions such as, "Where and how did humankind begin? What is the relationship to the god(s) of creation, what is man's final destiny and the meaning of life, suffering, and death?" There are hundreds of mythologies that show us how there was an evolutionary progression in the conception and fabrication of such gods seeking to obtain reassuring answers to these questions.[1]

Man makes gods of nature's powers

The first stage is today known among cultural anthropologists as "animism". Animism is the primitive belief that the forces of nature are attributed to one or various supernatural entities whose power cannot be equaled or be dominated by man. We have historical records from the Early Ages of humankind's development that refer to the existence of these gods. These numerous documents date back to the dawn of humanity when man learned to record his attempts to explain major life questions, such as the beginning of the universe, the existence of good and evil, the origin of life, injustice, man's capacity to

---

[1]   Joseph Campbell is probably one of the best interpreters of the function and significance of myths in man's evolutionary history dealing with the perspective of symbolic knowledge and its relation to the transcendent. His books are essential to understanding the complex way by which man processed and related to that mysterious reality of the Invisible, the Intangible, and the Incomprehensible.

do evil unto others, the reason for living, the possibility of life beyond the grave, and the existence of gods.

Historians tell us that the process of conceiving the existence of gods was a natural one, when our ancestors, much like us today, witnessed the frightening natural phenomena of an electrical storm ripping across dark skies, or the deafening roar of thunder that threatened to destroy the eardrums, or the fury of a storm whose hurricane winds were capable of ripping off the tops of trees dozens of meters tall as if they were grass blades plucked by two angry fingers. They, like us, witnessed how torrential rains caused rivers and lakes near their homes to overflow, pushing thousands of liters of water, and, with unstoppable fury, burying all in the way of its deadly path. And what can we say about those who were present when an uncontainable river of lava from a volcano burned, melted, and dragged everything in its wake, without the opportunity to flee quickly enough from the avalanche of devouring flames. Our remote ancestors panicked when the uncontainable and devastating force of an earthquake opened profound chasms swallowing forever those who fell in while their homes, tents, and huts collapsed like eggshells. They trembled with uncontrollable anguish when they heard the raucous rage of a roaring earth that threatened to annihilate every living creature.

Facing these portentous phenomena that raised panic, uncontrollable fear and reverence toward such deadly forces, men of the time, who did not have the scientific knowledge to explain them, attributed these powers of nature to superior beings who became the 'gods of nature'. We find them named as the sea-god, the storm-god, the water-god, the sun-god. Names of such gods abound among ancient tribes in all civilizations: the god of thunder and rain was called Tlaloc by the Aztecs and Bhagavataru by the Chenchus of the Hindu state, Andhra Pradesh; the god of wind was Quetzalcoatl to the Aztecs; the god of the angry sea for the Greeks was Poseidon; for the Incas, the god of earthquakes was Amaru; in Assyria, Adad was the god of weather.

Among the animist gods, the sun-god is the most important. He is perceived as the fountain of life on earth, responsible for the change of seasons and the warmth it bestows for things to grow. The worship of this great, powerful sun-god, reached the point in which small children were sacrificed to him, as was the case of the Canaanite god Baal during the time of the Hebrews (Jer.19: 5) and the sun-god of the Aztecs, in Mexico, many years later. (1)

Reverence toward these gods was expressed in many ways: dedication of sacred sites to specific gods with construction of lavish temples; developing rituals which included animal sacrifices, consecrated virgins serving in the temples; creating a priestly caste to ensure that the worship and offerings made to these gods were done correctly so that their objectives were achieved as to obtain their gods' blessings, offering them reverent submission, and appeasing their supposed fury against men.

Man Evolves from Animism to the gods of Olympus

From crass animism, where a deity was attributed to all natural phenomena, man entered a second stage wherein gods are created separately from the forces of nature with the power to control them. These gods, conceived in the "image and likeness" of man, have human characteristics. They are part of a family unit, have mothers, fathers, brothers, sisters. At this stage, these gods acquire super powers because they are in control of the forces of nature that threatened primitive man. They dominate the forces of nature, and manipulate them at will.

Among the powers attributed to the gods is the creation of the earth, animals, and humans. This power is described in hundreds of mythologies of past times and even recent ones. Two examples from a distant past prove how deeply rooted is the belief that man was created by a superior being. One of these myths is of Serbian origin. It states that in the beginning only God existed and that after He slept for a long time. He awoke one day and wherever He gazed, a star was born.

Admiring such beauty, He traveled and traveled until he arrived, hot and perspiring, on Earth where He paused. While resting a small drop of perspiration fell on the ground and from it, the first man was born. Because man was born from sweat, he was then condemned to a life of suffering and hardship. Another myth, told among the Lakota Indians of north and south United States, mentions the First Creator and the Lone Man--- both responsible for creating Earth and man. When Lone Man sees men suffering because of their hard lives, he decides to share their suffering, incarnating as man through an ear of corn that was being eaten by a young woman. (2)

At the same time, these gods that inhabit the heavens, behaved with the same human deficiencies. They were capricious, vengeful, egotistical, greedy, lecherous, scheming, liars, disloyal and treacherous. From their imperfect heaven, inaccessible to man who can only stare at it from Earth, these gods controlled the destinies of humans, even though they share the same limitations of those that created them in their own "image and likeness". That is to say, man can create gods that resemble him in all aspects, except for their immortality and power. Thus, the result is the appearance of imperfect gods with the same defects and passions as men's; gods who are more interested in the acquisition of power among the other gods and gaining celestial real estate than in the well being of mankind. In some mythologies developed by man, these gods created men to serve them, to work for them, as earth slaves. Men were also punished or harassed for transgressions the gods deemed unpardonable, such as Sisyphus who was condemned to push an enormous rock to the top of a hill, and, once there at the end of the day, the boulder rolled down to the bottom of the hill and he had to start the process over again. This punishment was imposed on Sisyphus because he convinced his wife not to follow the correct rituals for his burial; therefore, he was returned to Earth to fulfill them. Once back on Earth, Sisyphus evaded death. When the gods finally caught up with him, they decreed the punishment of pushing the rock up the hill over and over again, endlessly. (3) Interesting to note that this punishment for wrongdoing reminds us of the eternal punishment in hell for sins committed as was elaborated by Christianity into a dogma.

A brief look at three of the most well known civilizations - the Egyptian, Greek, and Roman - will allow us to see how the gods were conceived according to man's "image and likeness".

The Egyptians

Egyptian gods lived, hunted, fought, gave birth, ate, drank, died, and had human emotions. The realms of the gods sometimes overlapped and sometimes faded away. Which god ruled depended on the king at the time, where he wanted his capital to be, and which god he preferred. In the same manner, myths changed as the place where the gods were changed, as well as their names. Names in ancient Egypt were mystical and powerful. People then believed that if the name of an enemy was inscribed on an object that was then broken, this act would bring harm, and even death, to that enemy. If one knew the name, one had power over it. Each god had five names, each associated with an element, such as air, celestial bodies, or a phrase that describes a characteristic of the god, such as his virility or majesty.

The creator of all things was Ra, Amon, Ptah, Khunum or Aton, depending on which version of the myth had been adopted by the pharaoh of the time. Hathor and Horus represented the heavens. Osiris was the earth-god, as was Ptah. Hapi embodied the Nile's annual flood. Seth represented storms, evil, and confusion. His counterpart was Ma'at, who provided equilibrium, justice, and truth. Thoth and Khonsu were the moon. The sun-god, Ra, was seen in many roles and transcended the limits of the other gods. (4) This is Another good example of how the forces of nature were also considered to be gods.

Another good example of human passions projected unto gods is Horus, the falcon god, who was son of Isis and Osiris (both children of the supreme gods, Nut and Geb – which in itself is a projection of the reproductive capability of humans to beget sons).

Horus was the sworn enemy of Seth, who killed Osiris. Horus and Seth engaged in an endless battle. Isis was able to trick Ra, the sun god, into revealing his secret name for her, thus making her immortal. (5) Trickery, a human trait, is projected unto the gods.

The Greeks

The Greek Parthenon became one of the most elaborate kingdoms of the gods. A single query on the Internet returned 18 pages with more than 100 names of gods, goddesses, muses, monsters, Pleiades, and furies invented by people of that time. (6) The Greek gods displayed the same level of human passions as did the Egyptian gods.

Among the most well known was Zeus, who was the supreme god among the gods in Olympus. He was the father of heroes Perseus and Heracles. But Zeus had his own origin. He was the youngest son of the Titans, Cronos and Rhea. When Zeus was born, his mother, Rhea, hid him in a cave of Mount Dicte in Crete, in order to prevent his father, Cronos, from eating him as he had done with his siblings Poseidon, Hades, Hestia, Demetrius, and Hera. This is certainly one of the crudest conceptions of a father-god, who is so afraid of his own sons overthrowing him, that he eats them up as soon as they are born. Celestial cannibalism as its best. When he grew up, Zeus forced his father to throw up his brothers and sisters (justice is applied on the murderous father). They became allies and dethrone their father and the other Titans, imprisoning them in Tartarus, the subterranean world. Afterwards, Zeus splits creation with them. Poseidon keeps the kingdom of the waters and sea, Hades, the underworld and Zeus, the heavens, where he ruled with supreme authority. (7)

Once established as supreme god, Zeus continues to behave as humans do. First, he decides to eliminate any potential rival by killing the Titans and beginning anew. Prometheus, one of the Titans, has great affinity for humans and, when he becomes aware of Zeus' intentions, helps humans by giving the gifts of thought and fire, teaching them how to use it to cook and keep warm in winter. Zeus reacts angrily and chains Prometheus to a rock on the mountain where he is attacked daily by an eagle that rips off pieces of his liver. Every night Prometheus is healed, and each following day, the eagle returned to torment him. Zeus finally releases Prometheus when he tells him a secret about Thetis, the sea nymph, whom Zeus wished to wed. Instead, Thetis marries a human, King Peleus, a union that produced Achilles, hero of the Trojan wars. Zeus then cheats on his wife Hera with a mortal woman, Ateme, who gives birth to Hercules. When he grows up and find out his origins, Hercules not only defies Zeus' authority but has to be constantly on alert to avoid Hera's efforts to destroy him. (8)

This is an excellent scenario that showed how the 'heavenly gods' behaved displaying the worst of human passions: their greed, conflicts, emotions, fears, and worldly desires. The unique difference of these gods with humans was their overwhelming power, so many times used against the humans they despised, enslaved, and manipulated.

The Romans

Mars was considered the first major god of the Romans. The second force, Quirinus, was later identified as Romulus, the legendary founder of Rome. The third inhabitant of the Capitol Hill was Jupiter, who became supreme god, much like the Greeks' Zeus. Jupiter was also the protector of the city and its moral code, overseeing promises and treaties.

Among other prominent gods were Janus, the spirit of entrance of the door, and Vesta, the goddess of hearth and home, whose temple was guarded by Vestal Virgins. Gods with special abilities, such as Minerva, goddess of wisdom, arts, warfare and patron of craftsmen, were highly regarded. Hercules, the most popular demigod, was known for his labor, practicality, and defense of the oppressed. Mercury was associated with merchants, Fortune with fertility and Diana, the huntress, with wild animals and woodlands. (9)

Just as humans exhibited a sense of humor, so did the gods they created. Mischievous, roguish god Cupid is known as the god of love, shooting arrows at humans who immediately fell in uncontrollable love. Diana, the huntress, is the protector of young women. When she was seen bathing by Acteon, a hunter, she reacted in anger and turned him into a deer, which in turn was ravaged by his own hunting dogs. (10)

Once more, we can see clearly how another civilization projected unto the gods the array of human deficiencies, emotions, and passions making them truly in the 'image and likeness' of the men that created them.

Other Mythologies

It merits citing briefly other mythologies from other parts of the world as evidence of the human passions that were carried over to the realm of the gods.

In India, the legend described that Parvati, wife of the god Shiva, yearned for a child. Shiva refused as he saw no reason to raise a child to pay him homage. Parvati insisted so much that Shiva finally granted her wish. Shiva took a portion of her dress and from it created the child. Parvati so dedicated herself to her baby that Shiva, feeling jealous and ignored, burned the child's head with his third eye. Parvati's pain was such that Shiva repented, and in doing so, gave the child the head of the animal he saw first, an elephant. From that point on, Ganesh is depicted with a human body and the head of an elephant. (11) Once more, a human negative trait, jealousy, is the cause of death and the birth of an abnormal creature, a person with the head of an elephant.

The Aztecs believed that their god, Quetzalcoatl, the serpent god, was fooled by his brother who could not bear Quetzalcoatl's upright behavior. The brother's trickery transformed Quetzalcoatl into a human. Such was Quetzalcoatl's shock at his new appearance that he asked for help from his friend Xolotl, the coyote, who then made him a costume from Quetzal feathers. The custom made him look like a plumed serpent. Once more, Tezcatlipoca, his brother, tricked Quetzalcoatl. This time, the brother got him drunk and persuaded him to have intercourse with his sister. When Quetzalcoatl realized what he had done, he sacrificed himself, setting fire to himself on the beach. From there, he descended to the world of the dead where he asked permission from his father to extract the bones of the deceased in order to create humans. This permission was granted. Quetzalcoatl taught humans how to cultivate maize (corn) and other foods, to polish jade, to knit, to measure time, and to understand the meaning of the stars. (12) In this myth there is a strong hint that human qualities were stimulated in men by the god Quetzalcoatl, a different approach from other myths in which the gods behave negatively as humans do.

In Iranian mythology, the supreme god, Ahura Mazda, had a twin, Ahriman, who was in constant jealousy with his brother Ahura especially for giving birth to the beauty of Creation. In a jealous rage, Ahriman attacked Creation with hunger, lust, pain, sickness, even death. To prevent Ahriman from doing more damage, Ahura Mazda chained him to the very end of time. Despite the fact that Ahura Mazda makes men healthy and good, Ahriman infects them with sins, sickness, and sorrow. (13) Another example of the wrath of a god that inflicts hunger, lust, pain, sickness, even death on creation much the same way man inflicts these on other men.

Mythologies that describe the gods, who controlled nature, natural occurrences, and the lives of men, are clear evidence of man's limitations to conceive God. The best he could do was to create gods in his own "image and likeness" who were mere replicas of his own imperfections and virtues, but elevated to super powers. These supernatural beings in their distant heaven delighted, exalted, and glorified their existence, while men presented to them their plights and needs. From their heavenly abode these gods, according to their whimsical state, granted, or not, man's requests. Normally, the gods' responses were usually the same type of man's response on earth to his fellowmen.

The Bah'i Faith affirms that God has always spoken to humanity ever since it was able to listen to a Messenger of God. They have guided humans in their material and spiritual development, but unfortunately, we do not have historical records to know exactly who they were and what they taught. Baha'u'llah's (the founder of the Bahai Faith) great grandson, Shoghi Effendi, reasoned the phenomena in this manner:

> **"Regarding your questions: the only reason there is not more mention of the Asiatic Prophets is because Their names seem to be lost in the mists of ancient history. Buddha is mentioned, and Zoroaster, in our Scriptures -- both non-Jewish Prophets or non-Semitic Prophets. We are taught there always have been Manifestations of God, but we do not have any record of Their names. (14)**

So it would not be a surprise if historians discover evidences that several of the creation myths or the description of the gods living in the heavens may have evolved from original teachings given by a Messenger of God. As it has been recorded, myths evolve over time and end up not resembling much to the original story. This may have happened to the original teachings of the Messengers that through multiple interpretations and oral traditions were slowly transformed into the mythologies that we know today.

The fundamental question about what happens after death

Our ancestors asked many fundamental questions. Confronted with the blunt reality of physical death experienced on a regular basis, early man soon asked the crucial question, "What happens to man when he dies?"

The many answers to this question soon became complex diverse legends and mythologies arose similar to those that attempted to explain the gods of nature. From the moment that man began to use his rational powers, he had the intuitive knowledge - or illusion - that the loved ones who had died did not disappear when the body decomposed in its tomb. This intuition, this desire to not accept physical death as the ultimate disappearance of the loved ones led our ancestors to formulate the belief that when an individual died to this corporeal level, he/she crossed to the other side of Life to continue his/her existence.

In his first attempt to interpret this transition, ancient man ingeniously believed that upon death, the same elements that had permitted him to live on earth were required when he arrived on the afterlife. For this reason, prehistoric tombs (35,000 - 8,000 years ago) in Africa and Asia Minor contain bodies buried with ornaments, headdresses, weapons, and evidences suggesting that food was also included. The reason why the dead were dressed in fine clothes and ornaments, and were buried with the instruments they used in this life was because those remaining alive firmly believed that the dead would need them in their next live, which they believed that in some manner it was similar to the one lived here.

The Egyptian, Aztec, and Maya civilizations buried the dead body with personal belongings that they deemed would be useful in the afterlife. Items commonly placed within the tombs included axes, clubs, eating utensils, and often, dried food such as maize, beans and dehydrated potatoes. The most common adornments were animal teeth, shells, and above all, the canine teeth of deer, as discovered in a burial site at Arcy-sur-Cure, France. (15) Besides being buried with these needed artifacts, burials followed specific rituals, such as placing the body in fetal position, inside a pit or a jug or lying in the grave as if it were "sleeping". Each different ritual was a way of showing reverence for the departed and its elaborateness depended on the social status of the person while alive. Some cultures, such as the one imposed by the Pharaoh in Egypt, went to the extreme of burying the dead of high standing within the community with their favorite animals, such as dogs, and, in extreme cases, family members or personal servants.

The Egyptians believed that the deceased was carried to the other side of the river, the west bank, where Osiris, the god of death, would meet him. In a similar fashion, the Greeks believed that the realm of the death was found in the west of the world of their time. According to Greek mythology, Caronte, the boatman of Hades, is in charge of guiding the errant souls of the recently deceased, from one side of the Aqueronte River to the other, as long as they had the money to pay for the ride. This was the reason why in ancient Greece the dead were buried with a coin under the tongue in order to cover Caronte's fee. (16) The Italian poet, Dante Alighieri, immortalized Caronte in his extraordinary poem, *the Divine Comedy*, when he hands the boatman his coin in order to cross the river and begin his journey through the various levels of Hell.

What remains from these and other mythologies is the big question they asked about what happens to an individual when he dies. Did he keep on living or not? Did his existence continue in another dimension? Many of the mythologies expressed, in one way or another that an individual, upon death, continues to live on another level as a reward or punishment for his actions during his worldly life. The conception of punishment varies, but is the basis for the concept and image of Hell preached by Christianity. Even names attributed to Hell derive from civilizations that accepted this idea. For example, "Sheol" in Hebrew refers to the gathering place of all dead and "Hades" is the place where the dead of the Greeks go. (17)

Man's constant pre-occupation with the issue as to what happens after death becomes one of the central themes present in several of the well known Revelations made to man which has helped to appease this anguishing question. Once more, the alternate explanation can be included. That is, that it is highly feasible that originally Messengers of God gave the first notions of the afterlife in a very symbolic or metaphorical language, as they have frequently used in the past, and man, in his effort to understand these explanations, created the afterlife mythologies that we know today. They could have received the core teaching of an afterlife by one of these unknown messengers of God and afterwards used their own man-made images to explain, represent, and express such unknowable reality.

Nature's innermost organization

If man's preoccupation about life after death had anything to do with the creation of gods by men, so did the organization, the richness and variety of animal and plant species, the beauty of multicolor vegetation and flowers, the explosion of color at sunset, the incredible richness of fruits, the cyclical change of seasons. None of these splendid manifestations of nature could happen by chance, so it became necessary to introduce the presence of a Being with the incredible capability to 'invent' so much order and innate laws visible in Nature.

This need for affirmation becomes stronger and necessary as meteorological observations increased; as stars, seasons were studied, and winter, spring, summer and autumn cycles were observed. Cycles of rain and drought were also noted; exact times for planting and harvesting were established; high and low tides were verified. Then, as now, man was conscious that he was not in control nor did he direct such phenomena. Nature was in charge, with such precision and regularity that he was able to organize his life around sowing, harvesting, hunting, home building and management of water sources. Based on this regularity, man was able to plan his survival, to grow and develop the great civilizations we know today.

The regularity of the different cycles of Mother Nature led men to reflect and affirm that such order and regularity in nature must be the result of a Superior Mind, a Supreme Organizer, with the capacity, not only to conceive such order but, to make it happen at a planetary level. For humanity to conclude that there was a Superior Being was the outcome of logical reasoning, as was the case of the Greek philosopher, Aristotle (384–322 BCE), considered to be one of the greatest thinkers in antiquity. His well-known cosmological argument states that events precede each other, and, as such, change. Therefore, change happens. Change and time are everlasting; for there to be a change or eternal motion, there must exist an eternal substance capable of effecting the change. Since the causal argument cannot be applied indefinitely, it is necessary to pose the existence of an initial motor, a First Cause, the origin of motion, that does not depends on anything for its existence. (18)

This outstanding example of logical thinking did not impede many contemporary cultures at that time to believe that there were different and specific 'spirits' in nature. As such, they affirmed that there was the 'spirit' of the tree, of the water, of the mountain, of the wind, of each animal. They believed that these 'spirits' guided and dictated the behaviors and responses of the animal, plant or natural phenomena.

The motor conceived by Aristotle is an immaterial, unalterable force. The principle is the foundation of all motion, the ultimate cause of all that occurs on the planet. (19) This is undoubtedly a philosophical affirmation as to who God can be that surpasses mythological descriptions developed by civilizations preceding Aristotle. From concrete gods, conceived in an "image and likeness" of man, humanity moves to a non-material, non-temporal transcendent entity. God's Messengers revealed, each one in its own time, that man, is the one created by God in His own "image and likeness".

Despite Aristotle's advanced concept of a First Motor, undetached from all that has movement, he never postulated the existence of a Supreme Being, Everlasting and Autonomous, who was the Beginning of all that is. This is an affirmation, initially revealed to humans by God, not something deduced by man, even of Aristotle's caliber. The Messengers of God, who gave rise to today's known religions, revealed to Humanity this aspect of the essence of God. Thousands of years before Aristotle, Hinduism, Judaism, and Zoroastrianism, affirmed that

———

God was the Creator of all that exists by virtue of His Self-subsistence, His absolute power, and His ultimate wisdom.

Could Aristotle have heard the essential affirmation of God's Absolute Autonomy, His Ever- lasting Existence above which there is no other god, from the Jewish affirmations? There is suspicion that Socrates, Plato's teacher, who in turn taught Aristotle, traveled to the Holy Land where he certainly would have heard this affirmation about God. Socrates would have shared such knowledge with his disciple Plato, who in turn most likely would have shared it with Aristotle. Besides, the Jews of that time maintained strong commercial ties with various Mediterranean ports, including the port of Cyrene, Libya, which was very near where Aristotle's lived. (20)

Communication of philosophical or similar new ideas was in large part due to the merchant traders who either communicated them verbally or sold books containing these ideas to the cultivated Greek elite, always eager to be up dated in the latest ideologies. Through this channel of commerce, it is then quite possible that the Jewish ideas about God would have reached Greece. It is then conceivable that Greece, boasting that it was the birthplace of knowledge of the Mediterranean world, must certainly have known about the Jewish religion in existence for over 1,500 years.

Man cannot know the Essence of God

If something remains clear in this brief summary about how man has attempted to describe the gods he himself has conceived, it is that man, despite his formidable inquisitive capacity, is incapable of formulating, describing, elucidating, and affirming the essence of God in a manner that leaves no doubt that what he states Who God is, is in fact what He is. But, as we previously stated, man is limited and is incapable of knowing the Nature or the Essence of Who created him. It is above human's knowledge, and existence. Intimacy with the Creator is highly imperceptible, very mysterious, much like the intimacy that an individual can have with another individual. No one really knows a friend so well that he can affirm he has full knowledge of who the friend is. He cannot, because he does not even know himself completely. Knowing anything about God is a never-ending process of discovery that becomes more profound and enlightened as the individual enters higher levels of self-awareness and collective conscience.

This mysterious and revealing path is built slowly, gradually, as the individual goes through the various stages of biological growth, psychological development, and intellectual learning. No common man is born knowing who he is, the reason for his being or what will be his mission in his lifetime.

Why was I created? It is a question one must ask throughout one's life; a journey that has no immediate answer and no end. Thinkers are always discovering new facets, new dimensions as to why we were created. This is part of the adventure that Life offers us, the gentle, daily discovery of our potential, capable of bringing out the best in us for both our benefit and the benefit of those around us. It is a never-ending process that is not completed during our temporary existence on Earth.

Since process of self-discovery is slow, progressive, and un-ending for each individual, one can be certain that an individual cannot intimately or exhaustibly know God. To pretend that there is someone who knows the Essence of God, while not knowing his own essence, is basically a contradiction. Therefore, who can, without a shadow of a doubt, know what makes up God's Essence?

To be able to state or affirm that someone has that intimate knowledge about God is equivalent to saying that such individual is in some manner equal to God, because Only God knows completely and exhaustibly His own intimacy. This would be a new contradiction, since a created being can never know the nature or the essence of He who created him. His intellectual capability would not have such power. This is above his human capacity as a created being. Being a creation, no one can comprehend, understand, or become the autonomous Creator of all that is. Anything someone wishes to affirm about such Creator will be an approximation, a deduction, a supposition, not direct knowledge. Even then, whatever he affirms about the Creator, he cannot prove it directly, unequivocally.

God 'must' reveal Himself

If man does not have the capacity, knowledge, understanding, or the potential ability to know the Essence of Who God is, then, is there an alternative by which Man can get to know God? The alternative is that God, Himself, talks to man in a way that he can understand. But this implies that man's mind (originally designed by God) has an 'apriori' mental structure capable of acquiring some understanding, and comprehension of the Transcendent *when it is revealed* to him. Equally, that 'apriori' structure is able to intuit a level of certainty that such Revelation is truthful, that he is not being deceived, that his conclusions and reasoning about the Transcendent are valid. (21) Without this capability, man would not be able to grasp the content of God's Revelation. This assumes equally that, when encountering such a Revelation, man is not only able to understand it, but in the very act of comprehension, he transforms his spirit, his self-awareness of the relationship that binds him to his Creator. The grasping of the Revelation becomes the vehicle by which he enters into a transcendental relationship with the Creator Who has revealed Himself.

We must now determine if God has taken the initiative of revealing himself to mankind, telling them who He is and how we must understand Him. If this has happened we should ask, "How can God reveal Himself so that man can understand Him?"

Language, spoken, written, or symbolic, is the natural means of communication among men. Among all other attributes, this capability of communication is what makes man a true "creator". He becomes such when he is able to articulate ideas, feelings, emotions through words and images, be they spoken, written on paper, sung, or via paintings on canvas, figures carved on mud, forged in steel, molded in clay, embedded in plastic resins. All of these are the mediums by which man creates and shares his ideas with others. Man expresses his incredible creative capacity through language. Among all the components of language, the spoken word is the most commonly used.

If God wished to speak to us in a manner that we understood Him best, He would choose the most common, simple and universal vehicle: the spoken word. In order for God to "talk" to us, He must be able to express Himself verbally, in the same language as the one spoken by those who will hear Him. Without language, there is no possibility of communication. It is the natural vehicle that man uses to exchange ideas, to express his love, to recite beautiful poems, as well as, to insult and mistreat. Without language, man is indistinguishable from animals. Although animals do communicate through sounds, grunts, shrieks, and chemical signals, it is not human language. The major difference resides that human language is accompanied by an extraordinary ability to reason. This ability allows humans to comprehend thoughts and express them using symbols and words understood by others. A human is conscious of the fact that by creating concepts, not only can he express his thoughts, but, in doing so, can modify reality.

For us to understand God's essence, without falling prey to subjectivism, without fooling ourselves, without making mistakes, without supposing, without inventing His reality based on our imagination, as those civilizations we mentioned previously did, it is necessary to have another alternative; that is, that God talks to us, and tells us what He want us to know about His Essence. The most natural, comprehensible way for this to happen is for God to manifest himself in a human form, as an individual similar to us, who we can see, touch, and ascertain that he behaves like us. Using a human form, the Divine dimension, radically removed from us, becomes visible, tangible, and understandable. It is the inverse of the process we have seen before. If, in the past, man created gods in his own "image and likeness" in this new scenario it is God who presents himself to man, in the "image and likeness" of man. In the first case, divinity is defined by man; in the second, God, through His Spokesperson, communicates with humankind in their same language, allowing then to learn about His Essence and Divinity. By taking the initiative, God has eliminated the subjectivism of individuals who imagine God, using their limited mental capacity.

In revealing to man something of his Essence in a way that is comprehensible, God used the simplest means of understanding: the word, the foremost tool of human communication. But, He who speaks in the name of God cannot be just anyone. He must be an extraordinary being within whom the divine is present in such a manner that he is the Spokesperson of God. Thus, when this Messenger speaks, He does it in the name of God because, in fact, he is a perfect mirror of God's Attributes who speaks the eternal Word of God. Baha'u'llah, the founder of the Baha'i Faith, explains it in this manner:

> **"The door of the knowledge of the Ancient of Days," Bahá'u'lláh further states in the Kitáb-i-Íqán, "being thus closed in the face of all beings, He, the Source of infinite grace ... hath caused those luminous Gems of Holiness to appear out of the realm of the spirit, in the noble form of the human temple, and be made manifest unto all men, that they may impart unto the world the mysteries of the unchangeable Being and tell of the subtleties of His imperishable Essence... All the Prophets of God, His well-favored, His holy and chosen Messengers are, without exception, the bearers of His names and the embodiments of His attributes... These Tabernacles of Holiness, these primal Mirrors which reflect the Light of unfading glory, are but expressions of Him Who is the Invisible of the Invisibles." (22)**

This new explanation of the excellence of being of the Manifestation is still further expanded by 'Abdu'l-Bahá, the son of Bahá'u'lláh, who – having being authorize by his father to be the interpreter of his teachings - amplifies Bahá'u'lláh's thoughts with several additional nuances that complete the picture of the Manifestation's divine being, and yet not being God, the Unknowable Essence:

"As to the Holy Manifestations of God, They are the focal points where the signs, tokens and perfections of that sacred, pre-existent Reality appear in all their splendour. They are an eternal grace, a heavenly glory, and on Them dependeth the everlasting life of humankind. To illustrate: the Sun of Truth dwelleth in a sky to which no soul hath any access, and which no mind can reach, and He is far beyond the comprehension of all creatures. Yet the Holy Manifestations of God are even as a looking-glass, burnished and without stain, which gathereth streams of light out of that Sun, and then scattereth the glory over the rest of creation. In that polished surface, the Sun with all Its majesty standeth clearly revealed. Thus, should the mirrored Sun proclaim, 'I am the Sun!' this is but truth; and should It cry, 'I am not the Sun!' this is the truth as well. And although the Day-Star, with all Its glory, Its beauty, Its perfections, be clearly visible in that mirror without stain, still It hath not come down from Its own lofty station in the realms above, It hath not made Its way into the mirror; rather doth It continue to abide, as It will forever, in the supernal heights of Its own holiness. (23)

The response of those who listen and believe in the Manifestation as Messenger of God is to follow Him as disciples, who, in turn, spread the Revealed Word. In the beginning of mankind, there was no written language; thus, the Messenger traditionally transmitted the Revelation of God verbally. The transmission continued as oral tradition until centuries later it was finally consigned to papyrus, animal skins or scrolls, which then became known as the Sacred Books of that particular Revelation. Many years later, these Sacred Books were translated to multiple languages, making accessible the teachings of God to all those who could read, but who had not had the privilege of meeting the Messenger personally.

We can conclude that, for us to learn about the reality, the intimacy, the essence of God, objectively and genuinely, it is necessary that He reveals it unto us, because our limited understanding is unable to comprehend such reality. This has occurred in the past when God has taken the initiative to speak to mankind, through His Messengers, using the language of the group they spoke to so they could understand His Revelation.

This manner of learning about Who God is, what His essence is, is much more accurate and less bound by subjective, historical, and temporal interpretations of people imagining Who He might be. Anything that God reveals to us about Himself, when done through one of His Messengers, is guaranteed that whatever is revealed is closer to the truth of Who He is than any affirmation created by our imagination. Whatever God's Messenger affirms about who God is, arises from innate knowledge the Messenger has of who He is. The affirmation is not the result of personal efforts and collective attempts to define God; instead, it is the Revelation that God Himself has given us through His spokesperson, the Manifestation.

In what manner can we comprehend that the Divine presence can be made manifest within an individual? Is this possible? This is the core of the following chapters.

Chapter 1
References

Internet references are cited as I located them through Google. I am convinced that is easier for the reader if I provide the steps that I used to obtain them instead of only providing the technical reference. For example, http:// womenshistory.about.com/od/suffrage/

Not only is it cumbersome to type it in order to reach the site, but a slight mistake in one letter and the search fails. After many attempts, I decided that this is the simplest way to find the reference over again. Since this book is a translation from the original one in Spanish, some of the sources are quoted in Spanish because the data was found in such sites.

1) Google. Dioses del animismo. Wikipedia Encyclopedia. God of Animism
2) Neil Philip, *Book of Myths*, pg 17 y 53
3) Google. Sísifo, Enciclopedia Wikipedia Sisyphus
4) Google. Dioses egipcios de la antigüedad. Enciclopedia Wikipedia. Egyptian Gods of Antiquity
5) Neil Philip, *Book of Myths*, pg. 186
6) Google. Dioses griegos, dioses griegos. Greek gods
7) Google. Dioses griegos de la antigüedad. EnciclopediaWikipedia. Greek gods of antiquity
8) Neil Philip, *Book of Myths*, pg. 183
9) Google. Dioses romanos de la antigüedad. EnciclopediaWikipedia. Roman Gods of Antiquity
10) Neil Philip, *Book of Myths*, pg.182
11) Neil Philip, *Book of Myths*, pg. 144-45
12) Neil Philip, *Book of Myths*, pg 142-143
13) Neil Philip, *Book of Myths*, pg 30-31
14) from a letter written on behalf of Shoghi Effendi to and individual believer, dated 4 October 1950, in *The Compilation of Compilations*, vol. I, p. 22)

15) Google. Entierros primitivos. Los ritos funerarios prehistóricos | Historia de las Religiones www.historia-religiones.com.ar/los-ritos-funerarios-prehistoricos-5 Primitive Burials. Prehistoric burial rites -14

16) Google. Caronte (mitología) - Wikipedia, la enciclopedia libre es.wikipedia.org/wiki/Caront/mythology

17) Google. Sheol, Hades en Enciclopedia Wikipedia. Hades

18) Ask. Aristóteles. Aristotle, his philosophy

19) Google Aristóteles, Aristóteles. Biografía. ww.biografiasyvidas.com/monografia/aristoteles/ Aristotle. Biography

20) Bernard Grun, The Time Tables of History, pg 17; and Google. Cyrene, Lybia

21) Gustavo Baena, Fenomenología de la Revelación, pg. 59- 20

22) Shoghi Effendi, The World Order of Bahá'u'lláh, p. 113

23) 'Abdu'l-Bahá, Selections from the Writings of 'Abdu'l-Bahá, p. 49

Chapter 2

How Does God Reveal Himself?

In the previous chapter, we concluded that the common means of communication between humans is the spoken word. Therefore, if God wishes to communicate with humanity, if God wants to be understood as effectively as possible, the easiest way to accomplish it is by adopting a human form, and appearing as a real, live person, with a specific name, a line of ancestors, and a concrete family. As an individual He would grow up learning the same language as the one spoken by those whom He would address; He would be familiar with the details of their culture, their traditions, and their religion. He would also show typical human needs such as food intake, sleeping at night, wearing cloths, and bathing as well having intense human emotions such as pain, fear, and doubts.

In this way, God "adapts" His appearance and Revelation to the historical conditions being lived by the people He speaks to.

What are some of the characteristics and requirements that we would demand a person to have in order to accept him as a trustworthy, credible, and believable representative speaking in the name of God?

Requirements of God's Spokesperson

One of the first requirements is that, whoever will be speaking in God's name making a Revelation about Him, he does not appoint himself to carry out such a mission. This is a privilege reserved by God, who knows better than anyone, who is best suited to carry out such a delicate and sublime task. The appearance of the Manifestation is frequently surrounded by unusual events that suggest that this particular person is, since infancy, destined to carry out an extraordinary task. Later in his life, typically during his mature years, he affirms He is speaking in God's name and proclaims a new Revelation of God to the people He addresses.

There are hundreds of people who now and in the past have claimed to be speaking in the name of God, yet they have not met the aforementioned requirement. When this occurs, the individual manages to convince a group of followers to bestow on him such blind trust and obedience that they end up living in a cult. Whoever insists that he is speaking in the name of God, but cannot show any signs that he was selected by God for such a role, is usurping a position that is not his. By doing so, he cannot guarantee that what he claims to reveal is any more than a figment of his over-excited imagination and an illusion of his own creation.

Another requirement that we demand in order to accept this person as God's Messenger, speaking in His name and representing God on Earth, is an unblemished, moral and ethical life. He must display the embodiment of human virtues that are praised, exalted, and defended by the group to whom He is preaching. Only one that lives as he preaches acquires the right to be accepted, to be credible. The validity of what God wants to communicate must be supported by a spotless life, a path lit by the admirable qualities of all authentic prophets, and all messengers of divinity.

If there are contradictions, hidden or obvious, between what he preaches and the way he lives; if his individual behavior conflicts with what he preaches publicly, this individual is not credible; he cannot ascertain that he speaks in the name of God, because it is not acceptable that a representative of divinity should transgress the divine law he is revealing. A true Messenger of God private life must be spotless, coherent, unblemished, without contradiction with His Revelation. He maintains the message intact, defends it, and communicates it clearly, vehemently, and sincerely, independent of the adverse circumstances He may face affirming such Revelation. These circumstances includes persecution, defamation, incarceration, torture, mockery and public ridicule, exile, and, often, martyrdom.

A third requirement that a God's Spokesperson must have is that He has innate knowledge to understand who God is, in a way than no other mortal has. This allows Him to grasp the content of the Revelation He has being charged to deliver regarding the inner Essence of Who God is. The Spokesperson of God lives in an intimate and permanent communion with God, allowing Him to have an innermost knowledge of God that no human being could ever achieve. It is so intense, profound, and intimate that when He affirms anything about God, it is objective, real and valid. The presence of God within this individual is so strong and intense that we can unequivocally affirm that "God resides within him", making it possible to proclaim "God is present among us".

The Manifestation lives an unblemished lifestyle during His infancy, adolescence, and youth. At the appropriate moment of His maturity, He will proclaim His role and present himself as a Spokesperson, as a Messenger sent by God, announcing that He brings an explicit Revelation that God wants to share with all those willing to listen. But once again, it is necessary to emphasize that, for the proclamation to have credibility and be acceptable, the unblemished lifestyle of the Messenger must coincide with the message He will deliver. He must maintain integrity in his lifestyle throughout the rest of His life, regardless of the penalties, persecutions, and condemnations He may suffer for delivering such Revelation.

Has this occurred anytime during mankind's history? Has anyone appeared meeting the above-mentioned requirements? If yes, do we have documents, historical records or an oral tradition that validates His appearance?

Historical Evidence of These Messengers

The answer is "Yes". Historically there have been multiple Messengers who have given humans a Revelation in the name of God. Their initial followers presented the Revelation to those willing to hear it, who, in turn, have excited thousands of others to become followers and gradually His teachings have become a worldwide religion. This has happened because the followers have been fully convinced that the Revelation received was surely divine and, therefore, its tenets should be followed. What is remarkable is how all of the known worldwide Revelations answer the big questions humanity has posed since its appearance of Earth.

Who are these Messengers about whom we have concrete evidence of their existence and a record of their teachings either orally or written? They are:

- Krishna, who appeared in India around 3000 BC according to some historians and 1700 BC according to others. His teachings gave birth to the religion known as Hinduism, found mostly in India and Asia. It has become popular in the West through the practice of Yoga, created by Hinduism as a meditative discipline to achieve 'union with the divine'. Today it has approximately 900 million followers. (1)
- Moses, who lived in Egypt around 1,300-1500 BC, founded Judaism. Moses brought the Torah, known as the Law, cherished by Jews as a source of joy and blessing, but it has become a moral 'magna carta' for humanity. Judaism has today about 13.1 million followers. (2)
- Zoroaster appeared around 628 BC in Persia. His vision of God as the Creator of all that is good and Who alone is

worthy of worship became the basis of Zoroastrianism. Today it has approximately 2.6 million followers. (3)

- In India, Buddha appeared around 563 BC and His teachings on suffering and the end of suffering through inner and outer detachment became the basis of Buddhism. Today, depending on the source of information, it has somewhere between 230 and 1,691 million followers. (4)
- Jesus started his Mission around the year 36 of the Common Era and proclaimed to be the expected Messiah, but not a political one, rather a spiritual Messiah. His followers established Christianity, which today has approximately 2.136 billion followers. (5)
- The prophet Mohammed, born in the Arabian Peninsula, revealed himself around 622 CE, leaving His teachings recorded in the Koran. His followers created a complete empire based on Islamic law. It now claims to have 1.314 billion followers worldwide. (6)
- The most recent of these divine incarnations took place in Persia in 1844. A self-proclaimed divine messenger, known as The Báb, tirelessly announced the arrival of another Messenger greater than He, later known as Bahá'u'lláh, who in 1863 declared himself a Messenger of God. His personal writings are the basis of the Bahá'i Faith, which today has approximately 6 million followers worldwide. (7)

In the particular historical moment that each Messenger appears, His teachings slowly create a spiritual revolution among those who are willing to listen to him. A common characteristic of the above mentioned Messengers is that they speak about God and His transcendence, about creation, about the condition of humanity and its perennial questions in a way that their followers recognize that these Messengers are speaking in the name of God. They speak in such a manner that those listening to them are able to intuit that these Messengers have an experience of God so direct and intense that they speak with divine authority.

The Messenger Speaks in the Name of God

Those who have listened to these appointed Messengers notice that when They speak about God, They do so in His name, fully aware that They are His representatives. The Messenger is the Spokesperson of this mysterious Being whose essence they have been commissioned to reveal to those wishing to listen.

When a Manifestation appears at a determined point in time and place it is God communicating with man in the simplest and most efficient way that man knows: through the spoken word of a human being; in this case, His Messenger. In order to be understood, the Messenger speaks the same language of those He addresses at that moment.

Those selected Messengers become direct Spokespersons of God. They leave their teachings recorded within an oral tradition or a sacred book written by themselves, by their first disciples or later by their followers. The Messenger selected by God, when revealing something spiritual, supernatural, or some aspect of God's Essence, He does it in His name, as if God were speaking through him. If this were not so, it would not have the weight nor the validity that we demand from a Messenger of a Revelation. We accept and follow teachings if they come from God or His true Messenger, not from anyone who merely presents himself claiming to be enlightened or self-inspired, when in fact he has no evidence to back it up.

The question immediately arises, "Are these Divine Manifestations, displayed in human form, limited to the ones mentioned above?" Or can we assert that, ever since man appeared on Earth as a thinking, reflecting, and self-conscious being, from that moment on God has sent man an emissary who has spoken in His name? Have these Messengers given humanity the necessary guidance to continue evolving intellectually and spiritually? The scarce documents we have from ancient times are not sufficiently clear or precise to meet the requirements we now demand of historical records. Nevertheless, logic clearly suggests that, if God made man 'in His own image and likeness' (both affirmations made by many of the previously mentioned Spokespersons), He would not have forsaken man, His most precious creation. On the contrary, He would have continuously given guidance so that humanity would be able to walk the path of internal evolution, the dimension that makes man different from all other creatures, and the reason for God's special attention.

To this unique being selected by God to be His "official" Spokesperson, we will give a new name: that of "Manifestation" of God. With this word, we can distinguish Him from biblical minor prophets, from powerful spiritual teachers, from mystics and from gurus dedicated to internal growth through various spiritual disciplines. God's Manifestation is a special being, it is His representative, His spokesperson, His presence within the history of a specific people, bringing a particular Revelation about Himself and a renewed pact that shows His followers how to live according to new ethical, moral, and social norms.

The statement declaring that these are Manifestations of God (the mysterious Divine Presence among mankind) requires a more in-depth explanation. In our next chapter, we will try to clarify how it is possible for God to manifest Himself within a temporal space-time dimension, when He, Himself, is not constricted by these boundaries.

Chapter 2
References

1) Google. Hinduistas en el mundo, Enciclopedia Wikipedia Hinduists in the world, Wikipedia Encyclopedia
2) Google. Judíos en el mundo, Enciclopedia Wikipedia Jews
3) Google. Zoroastrianos en el mundo, Enciclopedia Wikipedia Zoroastrians
4) Google. Budistas en el mundo, Enciclopedia Wikipedia Buddhists
5) Google. Cristianos en el mundo, Enciclopedia Wikipedia Christians
6) Google. Mahometanos en el mundo, Enciclopedia Wikipedia Mohammedans
7) Google. bahai.org

Chapter 3

How can God appear among us?

The conclusion of the previous chapter raises the logical question, "How is it possible for God to manifest Himself within a temporal space, when He, Himself, is not constricted by time or space?"

God the Creator

There is an assumption that we must clarify. In order to affirm that God is not bound by space and time, we must have the certainty that God, by essence, is Infinite, does not occupy space or is determined by it; He is the Unrestricted. Moreover, He does not owe His Existence to anyone or any other cause. He is, by essence and definition the Self-Subsisting, not needing a cause for his Existence or Being. On the contrary, He is the cause and origin of all that is.

This fact about the nature and essence of God is not a conclusion that man arrived at through his own deductive efforts. Instead, it is a truth revealed by God through his Manifestations. The one most well known by the Western World comes to us through Christianity, who adopted the Old Testament of the Jews as an integral part of its sacred text, the Bible. That Manifestation was Moses. When he asked God how to respond to the Israelites, if they were to ask him the name of whom he spoke to on Mount

Horeb, the mount of the Lord, God answered from the burning bush, "**I am who I am**" (Exo. 3: 13-14).

This is one of the simplest, yet most thorough, definitions of Who God is. With these five words, God gave man one of the deepest truths regarding His essence. "I am who I am" is the same as "I am He Who has always been" --- thus, neither time nor space apply to Him. If time and space are not applicable, neither are source or origin, which is equal to saying that God has no beginning (not being created, He has always been) and no end (temporality does not apply). This is equivalent to being Self-subsisting, which means that His existence does not depend on anything or anyone. He is the Being. He is Existence. He is the beginning of everything that is; nothing not anyone originated Him. He is the Fountain of everything that is.

The affirmation that God is the Creator of all that was, is and will be was revealed at the beginning of time by the first Manifestations that appeared on Earth and has been reiterated by each subsequent Manifestation. So, in Hinduism, Brahma is the God of Creation, the Absolute God. In some Hindu traditions, He is considered a member of the trilogy along with Vishnu, the all-pervading God (the Preserver, in the form of kindness) and Shiva, the God of Destruction (in the form of ignorance). Nevertheless, being the Creator, Brahma conceives his children (Manas Putra or mind-children), demonstrating in this manner that their birth happens in the mind of Brahma (his creative attribute) and not via physical conception. Brahma is beyond description, manifestation, and the limitation of form, time or space. He is Eternal, Infinite, and Permanent, Knows all, and is Omnipotent. (1) This concept places Vishnu in the self-sustaining category. Although this symbolic description evades the concept we have in the West of one God Creator, it still confirms Hinduism's belief in a God, creator of the universe and man.

Buddha did not speak of God in Western terms. He probably did not describe Him in the same manner as other Manifestation such as Moses, Jesus or Mohammed did because he was born into a people and Hindu culture already populated by hundreds of gods, omnipresent in their homes, in neighborhood altars and in businesses. Nature was full of gods that represented God's qualities as if they were specific incarnations. Thus, for example, Agni is the god of fire, Surya is the sun god, Varuna represents the sky (atmosphere), Vayu is the wind god, and Kuberaq is the god of wealth. (2)

It seems that Buddha opted not to give a name to that divine reality, but instead to refer to it as the Source of all that is. His followers then attributed to him God's countenance so that Buddha was no longer a specific human being but an illumination. Buddha's body is the same illumination; therefore, Buddha will never disappear as long as the illumination exists. Buddha transcends all human thoughts. He is the perfect illumination, the Omniscient. (3) Within him meld Compassion and Wisdom. It is impossible to describe all attributes of the eternal Buddha, in so far that He does not have fixed characteristics; He can manifest any of them. (4) Buddha's true being does not appear or disappear. (5) Buddha is the father of all mankind, all men are His children. (6) He shows his followers the way to end suffering via eight noble paths: right view, right intention, right speech, right action, right livelihood, right effort, right mindfulness, and right concentration. (7) It is the means by which one can reach the state of illumination, and, in turn, arrive before the presence of He from which all emanates. As one can see, it is the path of life that allows a follower of Buddha to achieve that state of Nirvana, where all suffering disappears when the individual detaches himself from all that causes him pain, anguish and suffering. It is only when the individual is totally empty that Being can completely fill him.

The Old Testament of the Bible covers thousands of years of the history of the people of Israel. In Genesis, the first book, we have an extraordinary narration of the origins of the universe and man. In no uncertain terms, Genesis clearly states that the entire universe is the creative work of God, "**In the beginning God created the heavens and the earth**" (Gen.1:1). Similarly, it states that God created man in his own image and likeness:

"So God created man in His own image; in the image of God He created him; male and female He created them." (Gen. 1: 27)

The biblical story that continues in the following books is a constant reminder of man's condition as a created being and of God's role and autonomy with His creation. When Abraham confronts the king of Sodom, he does so under the warning "**I raise my hand to the LORD, Creator of heaven and earth, God Most High**". (Gen. 9: 22)

David, in many of his psalms, praises God's qualities but again re-iterates that God is the Creator of Nature, symbolized in the sun, the moon, and the stars.

> **"He made the great lights;**
> **His mercy endures forever!**
> **He made the sun to rule over the day;**
> **His mercy endures forever!**
> **And the moon and the stars to rule over the**
> **night. His mercy endures forever!"** (Psalm 136: 7)

Later, the apostle Paul, in speaking to the Romans, again reminds them of the creative power that belongs solely to God:

> **"For the invisible God, His eternal power and**
> **His divine nature, are made visible from the**
> **creation of the world; they can be understood**
> **by the things that are made, so that men are**
> **without excuse"** (Rom. 1: 20)

Mohammed repeatedly proclaims God the Creator of the Universe. Many of the Suras of the Koran allude to God's creative attribute. Let's examine two specifically. Sura 35 explicitly confirms God, the Creator, and the autonomy that He has over any other god:

1. "Praised be to Allah, Who created the heavens and the earth...He adds to Creation as He pleases: for Allah is Omnipotent".

3. O men! Call to mind the grace of Allah unto you! is there a creator, other than Allah, to give you sustenance from heaven or earth? There is no god but He: how then are ye deluded away from the Truth? (8)

The Sura of the Cow equally proclaims God as the Creator:

[2.21] "O men! worship your Lord, who created you and those before you, that you may become righteous.

[2.22] "Who made the earth a resting place for you and the heaven a canopy and (Who) sends down rain from the cloud then brings forth with it subsistence for you of the fruits; therefore do not set up rivals to Allah while you know". (9)

Bahá'u'lláh, God's most recent Manifestation to Humanity, whose followers practice the Bahá'i Faith, confirms over and over again God's rule and sovereignty over creation as can be seen in these selected of the many quotes from his writings:

"The purpose of God in creating man hath been, and will ever be, to enable him to know his Creator and to attain His Presence". (10)

"The incomparable Creator hath created all men from one same substance, and hath exalted their reality above the rest of His creatures". (11)

"Blessing be unto Thee, O Lord of Names, and glory be unto Thee, O Creator of the

heavens, inasmuch as Thou hast, through the power of Thy Name, the Self-Subsisting, given me to drink of Thy sealed wine..." (12)

Once established that God has revealed to us, via his Spokespersons, that He is who He is, that He is Everlasting and Eternal, the Self-subsisting, then the logical question ensues, "How can God, who is Infinite, who has no beginning or end, who is not restricted by space or time, be present in a concrete being, who is bound by space and time during his earthly life? How can Infinity fit into a human container, limited and finite?

The answer to this question becomes even more complex when Christianity defined as dogma that "Jesus was the Son of God (literally) and that God was composed of three entities, three persons---the Father, the Son, and the Holy Spirit. These three persons, although separate, shared the same divine nature, equally and eternally". (13) Theologians crafted this definition of the Holy Trinity in order to explain how God, being the Infinite, could appear in the space-time constrained individuality of Jesus, at the same time remaining the Infinite, Unconstrained God.

Is there another explanation, less difficult and complex, more logical and easier to comprehend?

Yes there is. It is not an explanation given by humans, but by Bahá'u'lláh, the most recent Manifestation of God to men, who wrote a book, *The Book of Certitude*, to explain this mystery. We will use it as an alternative explanation less difficult to understand and accept.

The Creative Word

An attribute of God that makes Him, who He is, besides His Self-subsistence and Eternity, is the attribute of Creator of all that is. He is the Creator or the Universe and all that inhabit it, including ourselves. The Word is the medium by which God's creative attribute is expressed. John, the Evangelist, at the beginning of his gospel, magnificently expressed this relationship between God, the Creator, and His Word:

"In the beginning was the Word, and the Word was with God, and the Word was God. The Word was in the beginning with God. All things were made by the Word; and without it nothing that exists was made". (Jn. 1: 1-3)

By means of this explanation, an essential identity between God and His Word is established because the Word is within God, it cannot be separate from Him, and is one of His attributes. The Word expresses He who utters it, because He who speaks it, owns it. Strictly speaking, the Word does not override its originator, because it is an attribute of Him; it is the most perfect expression of Who He is, as Creator, because "**all things were made by the Word.**"

The attribute by which God exercises his creative capacity is His Creative Word, eternal and ever-creating. For the Creative Word to be able to bring anything to the plane of existence, it is necessary that it partakes of the Knowledge of all that is. From this source, the Creative Word derives the power to create all that exists. This Eternal Word, this energy, this capacity, this aspect of God, this attribute of God, is perfectly present and expressed in the earthly reality of the Manifestation making Him a true Spokesperson in the name of God.

In man there is an analogous situation that can be useful to understand what we are trying to explain. Man is able to think an idea and convert it into a new tool, for example a metal cutter crafted with a laser beam. This tool is first conceived by an engineer as an idea. Possibly, the idea arose during a discussion as to how to resolve a practical problem: how to cut a very thick sheet of metal quickly, cleanly and without much effort. The idea finally dawns on him to use a laser beam as source of power in order to cut the metal. From there, he designs the machine on paper and, when he has detailed all of its components, he begins a process: first, obtaining or producing all the necessary pieces, then assembling the parts following his created blue print, fine tuning the new structure until the laser beam metal cutter has been crafted. He gives it an exotic and attractive name, "Selenetrix, the high power cutter." From that point on, in the world of construction engineers, the word "Selenetrix" will represent a laser beam metal cutter. The creative idea went from being an image to a concept, which generated a process that modified non-related objects and pieces (laser beam, electric cables, mirrors, optical lenses, screws, springs, tubes, metal rods, and pieces) into a new reality that did not exist. The pieces were assembled, put together according to a design and a new entity was born, the Selenetrix.

Man's creative word does not represent the totality of who he is. It is a faculty, a personal attribute of man, but it is not the person himself. When a word leaves his mouth and modifies reality in order to create something new that word remains as his personal attribute, even though that word has the power to create. It is the word that keeps the creative process going, but at no moment, the man that emits the word loses his individuality, his uniqueness which is always different, independent from the word that creates a new reality. He is present in the process directing the word, the concept and the idea that finally ends in the creation of the Selenetrix. Therefore, his creative word becomes manifest in the new reality that emerges, but at no time was such word the totality of the "I" that generated it. The creative word was the one that created a new reality. But the total "I" that constitutes the full reality of the engineer was not diluted at any moment in the idea that created the Selenetrix, although it was his word that gave existence to the new invention.

There is still another way one can comprehend how an individual can maintain his personal individuality while having multiple expressions of himself. All his involuntary functions (respiration, digestion, circulation, kidney functions, etc.) occur concurrently and automatically, without the individual having to worry that they have to occur constantly, as long as he lives. These involuntary functions are controlled by the part of the brain that regulates and keeps them functioning non-stop. Another part of the brain stores life experiences as memories that can be recalled from this archive at the moment when consciousness needs them. Similarly, there is another portion of the brain, which controls logical thinking and the construction of concepts; and yet another, that deals with imagination and artistic creativity. Sometimes, the same person expresses himself as father, other times as son, others as spouse, as friend, teacher, student, lover, benefactor, laborer, or professional. He is the same individual who manifests himself in different capacities, in different forms of being. Yet, these various expressions do not exhaust his individuality. He remains an entity independent of the multiple roles he assumes. But each role in itself is particularly unique and different from the other roles, although the same individual acts them all out.

Let us use another analogy, and, as such, it is just another approximation to help us further understand what we have been trying to explain. If we compare God to the Sun (this is the analogy), the Sun is continuously emitting revitalizing rays whose energy gives us life here on Earth. Let us say that some of the light beams singularly renovate life at the beginning of spring. These life-giving rays originate in the Sun, but it is not the Sun itself that reaches the Earth. The Sun remains where it is and it continues shining and emitting life-giving rays. At no point in time does it stop being the Sun that gives life to all living things on the planet and to all other planets that it blankets with its energy. When this happens on Earth every day there is a sunrise, it is as if the Sun itself appears on Earth in a way that benefits it; yet we know that if the Sun itself comes any nearer to Earth from where it is today, it would reduce the planet to ashes, evaporating it, destroying it with its overwhelming cosmic force. In order for it to give and sustain life on the planet, it is necessary that only a fraction of its energy reaches Earth. In a similar way, God (the Sun) emits His spiritual life giving spiritual life to man, which is channeled through the Revelation presented by the Manifestation, in His name.

When the Divine Word (the creative attribute, the beam of light that the Divine Sun emits) reaches man through the Revelation given by His Manifestation, then God Himself does not abandon or, for an instant, suspends being the Eternal, Unrestrained God. This perspective gives a new light and meaning to John's words: "**And the Word was made flesh, and dwelt among us**." (Jn.1, 14)

The Creative Word appears among men, in His Spokesperson, who communicates to man what God wishes to reveal about Himself through the particular Revelation made by that Manifestation. At the same time, the specific Revelation is the expression of God's Plan for man at the particular point in history when the Manifestation appears. Bahá'u'lláh, God's most recent Manifestation (1863) and founder of the Bahá'i faith, left for us in his *Book of Certitude* a full detailed explanation of the Manifestation's divine nature. He also let us know how the Manifestation speaks in the name of God:

> "**Through their appearance the Revelation of God is made manifest, and by their countenance the Beauty of God is revealed. Thus it is that the accents of God Himself have been heard uttered by these Manifestations of the divine Being**". (14)

Being that God's Word become audible via the Manifestation's human form, it has the strength, the power, the authority, the capacity to transform man's heart once it comes in touch with it. This contact can occur listening directly to the Manifestation while He delivers His Revelation or by coming into contact with the Word as recorded in the Sacred Book of each particular Revelation.

When this happens, the Manifestation, through whom God speaks, does not lose his individuality as a human being. Neither does He lose the psychological profile that identifies him as a unique and unrepeatable individual. His humanity is not nullified, because his human needs, such as sleeping, eating, walking, and bathing continue. Even the simplest of human functions, as digestion of food and other biological necessities, or feeling noble emotions such as compassion, tenderness, forgiveness, and charity also remain. If that were not the case, all Manifestations would have the same physiognomy, the same name, the same body, the same psychological make-up. As it is, what we observe is that all, being real men, are different, each with a clearly defined individuality. Bahá'u'lláh refers to this difference of individualities as differences of station (the Mission that each one has): **"It hath ever been evident that all these divergences of utterance are attributable to differences of station"**. (15)

Although none of the human characteristics are lost when Divinity manifests in the chosen individual, a radical transformation does occur in that person. He ceases to exist and live in the same plane of being as the rest of mankind and enters the plane of "divinity made present in human form". The Creator and the created have a symbiosis by which the appointed individual lives an existence in perfect communion with the Divine. His human life becomes completely immersed, bathed, and permeated by the presence of the Word. Bahá'u'lláh expresses this mysterious reality in the following terms:

> **"Thus, viewed from the standpoint of their oneness and sublime detachment, the attributes of Godhead, Divinity, Supreme Singleness, and Inmost Essence, have been and are applicable to those Essences of being** (the Manifestations)**, in as much as they all abide on the throne of divine Revelation, and are established upon the seat of divine Concealment"**. (16) [word in parenthesis included for clarity]

At the same time, a symbiotic process develops by which the will of the individual becomes one with the Will of God. His innermost self enters into communion with God at a level of intensity that no other human can experience. Bahá'u'lláh explains this symbiosis as follows:

> **"Whilst walking amongst mortals, they soar in the heaven of the divine presence. Without feet, they tread the path of the spirit, and without wings they rise unto the exalted heights of divine unity. With every fleeting breath they cover the immensity of space and at every moment traverse the kingdoms of the visible and the invisible".** (17)

The symbiosis becomes so perfect that when the Manifestation speaks about God, when He reveals something about His essence, when He explains anything about the spiritual reality after death, it is as if God Himself were speaking with a human voice and in human words. That is why, when the Manifestation reveals something of content, be it spiritual, supernatural or about God, He does so in the name of God, as if God were speaking through Him. Bahá'u'lláh describes this unfathomable reality as follows:

> **"He (God) hath manifested unto men the Day Stars of His divine guidance, the Symbols of His divine unity, and hath ordained the knowledge of these sanctified Beings to be identical with the knowledge of His own Self. Whoso recognizeth them hath recognized God. Whoso hearkeneth to their call, hath hearkened to the Voice of God, and whoso testifieth to the truth of their Revelation, hath testified to the truth of God Himself. Whoso turneth away from them, hath turned away from God, and whoso disbelieveth in them, hath disbelieved in God".** (18)

He reiterates this idea in another passage with a light variance:

> **"The Person of the Manifestation hath ever been the representative and mouthpiece of God. He, in truth, is the Day Spring of God's most excellent Titles and the Dawning-Place of His exalted Attributes".** (19)

In the Manifestation, the Divine is present in a manner and way that cannot be found in any other creature, or any other man. The Presence is so unique, that Bahá'u'lláh acknowledges that **"the attributes of God"** are present within these Manifestations in a sublime, extraordinary manner for they are **"Embodiments of the attributes of God"**:

> **"Nay rather, the attribute of sovereignty and all other names and attributes of God have been and will ever be vouchsafed unto all the Manifestations of God, before and after Him, inasmuch as these Manifestations, as it hath already been explained, are the Embodiments of the attributes of God, the Invisible, and the Revealers of the divine mysteries".** (20)

What the Manifestation expresses about God becomes Revealed Word. Whoever listens to it can be assured that whatever the Manifestation reveals is what God wishes to communicate to us, because it is the Divine Word that speaks through the Manifestation. In another passage of the same book, Bahá'u'lláh expresses this idea as follows:

> **"Furthermore, it is evident to thee that the Bearers of the trust of God are made manifest unto the peoples of the earth as the Exponents of a new Cause and the Bearers of a new Message. Inasmuch as these Birds of the Celestial Throne are all sent down from the heaven of the Will of God, and as they all arise to proclaim His irresistible Faith, they therefore are regarded as one soul and the same person. For they all drink from the one**

**Cup of the love of God, and all partake of the
fruit of the same Tree of Oneness".** (21)

It is important to pause for a moment and analyze the last phrase, **"therefore they are considered as one soul and the same person"** because it is the key to understanding how these Manifestations, each being a different individual can, nevertheless, be regarded as One and having the same origin. The Manifestation has its divine and unique origin in God, and God is One. Bahá'u'lláh explains this profound reality in the following poetic manner:

"It is clear and evident to thee that all the Prophets are the Temples of the Cause of God, Who have appeared clothed in diverse attire. If thou wilt observe with discriminating eyes, thou wilt behold them all abiding in the same tabernacle, soaring in the same heaven, seated upon the same throne, uttering the same speech, and proclaiming the same Faith". (22)

To help us further understand the mysterious divine oneness of all Manifestations Bahá'u'lláh reiterates the concept once more:

"Purge thy sight, therefore, from all earthly limitations, that thou mayest behold them all (the Manifestations) **as the bearers of one Name, the exponents of one Cause, the manifestations of one Self, and the revealers of one Truth, and that thou mayest apprehend the mystic "return" of the Words of God as unfolded by these utterances".** (23)

So, as to leave no doubt that these Manifestations originate in God, Bahá'u'lláh explains that precisely within them reside the divine Attributes to such a degree and perfections that they become God's Spokesmen:

"Thus, viewed from the standpoint of their oneness and sublime detachment, the attributes of Godhead, Divinity, Supreme Singleness, and Inmost Essence, have been and are applicable to those Essences of being, inasmuch as they all abide on the throne of divine Revelation, and are established upon the seat of divine Concealment". (24)

Since the divine origin of all these Manifestations is the same, a logical consequence of such Oneness is that each can affirm that He is the return of the previous Manifestation. Such affirmation is a simple conclusion based on the fact that the Manifestations all have the same divine origin. Bahá'u'lláh explains it in this manner:

"It is clear and evident to thee that all the Prophets are the Temples of the Cause of God, Who have appeared clothed in diverse attire. If thou wilt observe with discriminating eyes, thou wilt behold them all abiding in the same tabernacle, soaring in the same heaven, seated upon the same throne, uttering the same speech, and proclaiming the same Faith. Such is the unity of those Essences of being, those Luminaries of infinite and immeasurable splendor. Wherefore, should one of these Manifestations of Holiness proclaim saying: "I am the return of all the Prophets," He verily speaketh the truth". (25)

Jesus expressed the same premise when He affirmed "**Most assuredly, before Abraham was, I am.**" (Jn. 8: 58). By making this statement Jesus is saying that His existence as a Manifestation had always being in the spiritual realm as so had Abraham's being. Mohammed also made the same comparison when He stated "**For Allah, Jesus is similar to Adam, whom he created of dust, and then said He unto him, 'Be,' and he was**". (26) To understand how this happens in a concrete Manifestation, Bahá'u'lláh describes the unity that existed between Mohammad and Jesus:

> **"As to the matter of names, Muhammad, Himself, declared: "I am Jesus." He recognized the truth of the signs, prophecies, and words of Jesus, and testified that they were all of God. In this sense, neither the person of Jesus nor His writings hath differed from that of Muhammad and of His holy Book, inasmuch as both have championed the Cause of God, uttered His praise, and revealed His commandments".** (27)

In this way, there is continuity in the Word Revealed since each Manifestation, speaking in God's name, drinks from the same fountain of divine Knowledge, God Himself. Because they all have the same origin, they display to man a Revelation about the Essence and Will of God that neither contradicts nor denies what has been previously revealed. Generally, each subsequent Revelation provides a new vision; a new understanding of texts previously revealed or clarifies points that up until then remained unclear.

For this reason, in some sacred writings there are apparent contradictions between the affirmations made by a previous Manifestation and the following one. A content analysis, an understanding of the context in which the Manifestation delivers its affirmation helps us understand why there are differences or apparent contradictions. Bahá'u'lláh clarifies the discrepancy:

> **"It is because of this difference in their station and mission that the words and utterances flowing from these Well-springs of divine knowledge appear to diverge and differ. Otherwise, in the eyes of them that are initiated into the mysteries of divine wisdom, all their utterances are in reality but the expressions of one Truth. As most**

of the people have failed to appreciate those stations to which We have referred, they therefore feel perplexed and dismayed at the varying utterances pronounced by Manifestations that are essentially one and the same". (28)

If the various **"utterances pronounced by Manifestations that are essentially one and the same"** the apparent discrepancies of the Manifestations' Revelation are due to their 'station and mission', meaning that each one has had a distinct personality and a particular mission to accomplish. This in no way negates that they **"all abide on the throne of divine Revelation, and are established upon the seat of divine Concealment".** (29)

This is a summary explanation of how God's most recent Manifestation has illuminated our understanding of how God, Infinite, Uncreated, Eternal, can "be made manifest" among mankind as an individual, limited, created, without ever stop being the One God.

The Message brought by each Manifestation is the new Revelation that God wishes to communicate to Mankind and it does it through the Manifestation that presents a new Revelation to the specific group where it appears. Let us now consider what is the best way by which we can understand the Mission of the Manifestation, how similar it is to Missions of previous Manifestations and how it differs from them.

Chapter 3
References

Note: The majority of Bahá'i quotations that appear in this and subsequent chapters were obtained from texts found in OCEAN, the free program of the faith, which can be downloaded from the Internet (http://www.bahai-education.org). In said program, the principal books written by Bahá'u'lláh, 'Abdu'l-Bahá y Shoghi Effendi, main spokesmen of the Faith, are available. The number at the end of each quote refers to the page in which it appears within the program. I also used the Jerusalem version of the Bible, available on the Internet, as well as the King James Bible.

1) Google. Dios creador en el Hinduismo. Teología hinduísta-Taringa!*www.taringa.net/posts/imagenes/98389/Teologia-hinduista.html*

2) Google. Dios del hinduismo - Ecyclopedia Wikipedia, *wikipedia.org/wiki/Hindu_deities.*

3) *The Teaching of Buda*, pg. 66

4) *The Teaching of Buda*, pg. 50-52

5) *The Teaching of Buda*, pg. 62

6) *The Teaching of Buda*, pg. 68

7) José Luis Márquez, *Educadores de Humanidad*, pg. 88

8) Google.*Corán - Coran*.org.ar *www.coran.org.ar/-* Sura 35, 1,3

9) Idem, Sura 2, 21,22

10) Bahá'u'lláh, *Gleanings from the Writings of Bahá'u'lláh*, XXIX, p. 70

11) Bahá'u'lláh, *Gleanings from the Writings of Bahá'u'lláh*, XXXIV, p. 80

12) Bahá'u'lláh, *Tablets of Bahá'u'lláh*, p. 110

13) Google. Credo Atanasio. Enciclopedia Católica

14) Bahá'u'lláh, *The Kitáb-i-Íqán*, p. 177

15) Bahá'u'lláh, *The Kitáb-i-Íqán*, p. 177

16) Bahá'u'lláh, *The Kitáb-i-Íqán*, p. 177

17) Bahá'u'lláh, *The Kitáb-i-Íqán*, p. 66

18) Bahá'u'lláh, *Gleanings from the Writings of Bahá'u'lláh*, p. 48
19) Bahá'u'lláh, *Gleanings from the Writings of Bahá'u'lláh*, p. 68
20) Bahá'u'lláh, *The Kitáb-i-Íqán*, p. 106
21) Bahá'u'lláh, *The Kitáb-i-Íqán*, p. 151
22) Bahá'u'lláh, *The Kitáb-i-Íqán*, p. 153
23) Bahá'u'lláh, *The Kitáb-i-Íqán*, p. 159
24) Bahá'u'lláh, *The Kitáb-i-Íqán*, p. 177
25) Bahá'u'lláh, *The Kitáb-i-Íqán*, p. 152
26) Google. *Korán - Coran*.org.ar *www.coran.org.ar/*-Sura 3, 59
27) Bahá'u'lláh, *Gleanings from the Writings of Bahá'u'lláh*, p. 21
28) Bahá'u'lláh, *The Kitáb-i-Íqán*, p. 177
29) Bahá'u'lláh, *The Kitáb-i-Íqán*, p. 177

Chapter 4

The Manifestation's Mission

Summarizing the previous explanations

In the previous chapter, we saw how we can entertain the possibility that God, in order to speak to us, manifests in an individual. We made it clear it is not God, the Infinite, the Uncreated that appears in human form. The Manifestation becomes the resplendent mirror in which God's attributes, as His Creative Word, becomes audible for humans to listen. We call this historical presence, the Manifestation of God. Let's now see how one can understand the role that the Manifestation of God plays in the history of Humanity.

Each Manifestation is God's Spokesperson. He is God's presence among men addressing them in human form. This is why we can say that the Manifestation is the closest that men can "see" God, "hear" His voice, "listen" to His Revelation. Since the Manifestation is in perfect communion with God, understands perfectly what God wishes to communicate to humans at the time He speaks to them, at that moment, the Manifestation is no longer a common human individual. It is God's Word speaking to mankind. What the Manifestation reveals is, genuinely, the Word of God. Because God is speaking to man through His chosen one, at that moment that Word has the authority to speak in the name of God, as Bahá'u'lláh explains:

> **"Were any of the all-embracing Manifestations of God to declare: "I am God!" He verily speaketh the truth, and no doubt attacheth thereto. For it hath been repeatedly demonstrated that through their Revelation, their attributes and names, the Revelation of God, His name and His attributes, are made manifest in the world".** (1)

Similarly, Jesus confirmed this same reality when He said of Himself:

> **"What I say to you I do not speak of my own accord: it is the Father, living in me, who is doing his works".** (Jn. 14: 10)

> **"And the word that you hear is not my own: it is the word of the Father who sent me".** (Jn. 14: 24)

The Mission of all Manifestations

The Manifestations share the same Mission: to make man continuously conscious of the reason why he was created; that is, to know God, and attain his Presence. Bahá'u'lláh clearly reminds us that this objective has been recorded in all sacred texts:

> **"The purpose of God in creating man hath been, and will ever be, to enable him to know his Creator and to attain His Presence. To this most excellent aim, this supreme objective, all the heavenly Books and the divinely-revealed and weighty Scriptures unequivocally bear witness".** (2)

The fact that this goal of humanity has been recorded in the sacred books of the past religions implies the existence of previous Manifestations because, as it was explained above, the Manifestation is the author of the sacred text, regardless of whether His teachings were dictated or written by Him or they were transmitted by oral traditions.

Another aspect common among Manifestations is the delivery of a new Revelation that God wants His followers to hear and put into practice. Generally, this new Revelation redefines the agreement carried out by the previous Manifestation between God and the people He addressed. It is a reiteration of what has already been revealed about God by previous Manifestations, but at the same time it introduces one or various new aspects of God's "unknowable essence". It also proposes a series of laws for daily living, which address how to relate to God, and an ethical and moral code when relating to others.

Another element common to all Manifestations is the fact that God has two purposes in mind when sending His prophets to mankind. The first is to liberate the sons of man from the darkness of ignorance and guide them towards the light of true understanding. The second is to assure the peace and tranquility of the human gender, providing all the means by which they can be established. In this sense, the Manifestations act as the physicians of Humanity being capable of identifying the illness that mankind is suffering at that moment. As a spiritual physician, He can prescribe the best medicine to cure the illness. Again, Bahá'u'lláh states it in a way that requires no further explanation:

> **"The Prophets of God should be regarded as physicians whose task is to foster the well-being of the world and its peoples, that, through the spirit of oneness, they may heal the sickness of a divided humanity. To none is given the right to question their words or disparage their conduct, for they are the only ones who can claim to have understood the patient and to have correctly diagnosed its ailments. No man, however acute his perception, can ever hope to reach the**

heights which the wisdom and understanding of the Divine Physician have attained. Little wonder, then, if the treatment prescribed by the physician in this day should not be found to be identical with that which he prescribed before. How could it be otherwise when the ills affecting the sufferer necessitate at every stage of his sickness a special remedy? In like manner, every time the Prophets of God have illumined the world with the resplendent radiance of the Day Star of Divine knowledge, they have invariably summoned its peoples to embrace the light of God through such means as best befitted the exigencies of the age in which they appeared. They were thus able to scatter the darkness of ignorance, and to shed upon the world the glory of their own knowledge. It is towards the inmost essence of these Prophets, therefore, that the eye of every man of discernment must be directed, inasmuch as their one and only purpose hath always been to guide the erring, and give peace to the afflicted.... These are not days of prosperity and triumph. The whole of mankind is in the grip of manifold ills. Strive, therefore, to save its life through the wholesome medicine which the almighty hand of the unerring Physician hath prepared. (3)

The relationship of each Manifestation with His predecessor

Each new Manifestation that appears in history always has a link to the one that preceded Him because "**in every subsequent Revelation, the return of the former Revelation is a fact, the truth of which is firmly established**". (4)

This is why a new Manifestation often states that He is the return of prior Manifestations and affirms this because all come from the same origin, God. It is the deepest sense of the reply given by Jesus to the Jews who wanted to incarcerate Him for healing on the Sabbath, **"If you really believed him (Moses) you would believe me too, since it was about me that he was writing; but if you will not believe what he wrote, how can you believe what I say?"** (Jn. 5, 46-47); and by Mohammed who stated: **"For Allah, Jesus is similar to Adam, whom he created out of dust and to whom he said, 'Be', and 'he was'".** (5)

The unity that exists among the Manifestations allows any one of them to make such affirmation. Bahá'u'lláh recorded it thus:

> **"As to the matter of names, Muhammad, Himself, declared: 'I am Jesus'. He recognized the truth of the signs, prophecies, and words of Jesus, and testified that they were all of God. In this sense, neither the person of Jesus nor His writings hath differed from that of Muhammad and of His holy Book, inasmuch as both have championed the Cause of God, uttered His praise, and revealed His commandments".** (6)

In another section of the same text, Bahá'u'lláh reiterates the same idea,

> **"Wherefore, should one of these Manifestations of Holiness proclaim saying: "I am the return of all the Prophets," He verily speaketh the truth".** (7)

With respect to the content of the Revelation made by its predecessors, the new Manifestation validates all that the previous Manifestation has revealed about Who God is, how to comprehend His Essence, and what are the moral laws that will not fade because they are eternal. Thus, we can understand Jesus' affirmation when He stated: **"Do not imagine that I have come to abolish the Law or the Prophets. I have come not to abolish but to complete them"**. (Mt. 5, 17) The validation of what is permanent of the prior Revelation's is what seals its immutability. It confirms that it is not subject to man's capricious intents to change it when he interprets and reinterprets the Revelation according to his imagination and desires.

As each Manifestation brings a new Revelation, generally, it renews the prior Revelation, modifying it, enlarging it, repealing portions of it and creating new directives. This is possible and necessary according to the words of the founder of the Bahá'i Faith,

> **"Every Prophet Whom the Almighty and Peerless Creator hath purposed to send to the peoples of the earth hath been entrusted with a Message, and charged to act in a manner that would best meet the requirements of the age in which He appeared".** (8)

The Manifestation's mandate *"to act in a manner that would best meet the requirements of the age in which He appeared"* is the reason why the interpreters of the teachings of the Manifestations create the differences between religions making them appear as being irreconcilable. This separation is made acute when the followers enthrone the social and cultural aspects as the core of the new Revelation, rather than uphold what the Manifestation has revealed about God as the true essence of the new Revelation. For example, the "impure foods" defined by God in the Old Testament that were not to be eaten. At the time when God gave this mandate, the majority did not understand the reason for this request. It became clear centuries later when science verified that the prohibited foods are toxic, bad for our health and even create sickness, and, therefore, should be avoided. The fact that a Revelation prohibits certain foods, and a subsequent Revelation does not mention them, it does not mean that what the previous Revelation revealed about God is invalid. God's prohibition of eating certain foods is important because if comes from God, but it is not essential to what the Revelation has said about Who

He is. Therefore, the prescription regarding foods is relative and modifiable, if the subsequent Manifestation deems it so.

The social phenomena of slavery is an excellent case in point. Before Bahah'u'lláh, neither Moses, nor Buddha, nor Jesus declared that God wanted man to abolish slavery, which was so prevalent as a human behavior throughout most of the world. The absence of such prohibition does not mean that the Manifestations justified the cruelty or the abuse of slaves as was so common. Such justification would have been contrary to the teachings of all Manifestations even without abolishing the system of slavery itself. There are multiple reasons for the existence of slavery that was present worldwide since over 5,000 years ago. Of the many that can explain the appearance of slavery, most historians agree that slavery acted as the backbone of the economic systems of the empires during those years, and the building of a world economy. (9 – see reference of some of these authors)

Slavery lasted so long that it was not officially abolished in the United States until December 18, 1865, upon the approval of the 13th Constitutional Amendment at the end of the Civil War. This happened after 3.5 million blacks were forcibly removed from their homes in Africa and shipped as cargo-slaves to the North American colonies and the Spanish Central and South America colonies under such inhuman conditions that as many as one-third perished during the ocean crossing. (10) The majority of these slaves were bought by wealthy landowners to work the cotton and tobacco fields in North America and the banana, sugar cane, and cocoa plantations of the landowners of the Caribbean, Central America, and Brazil; and the silver mines of Peru. Their inhuman living conditions were the cause of thousands of them dying from diseases, malnutrition, and unsanitary living quarters. (11)

Bahá'u'lláh forcefully declares in the Kitáb-i-Aqdás, His Book of Laws, that slavery is no longer accepted by God when He states:

"It is forbidden you to trade in slaves, be they men or women. It is not for him who is himself a servant to buy another of God's servants, and this hath been prohibited in His Holy Tablet". (12)

This is a new social commandment based on the definition of equality of all men and women before God. In a sense, it is an advance over previous Revelations because it modifies a conduct that until then was legally and morally acceptable, and not prohibited by prior Manifestations. This had not happened because, in the word of Jesus, **"I still have many things to tell you, but you can't bear them now."** (Jn, 16, 12)

The uniqueness of the Revelation of each Manifestation

At the same time that there are these common elements to all Manifestations, there are also concrete differences among them. They arise by the fact that each Manifestation is a different individual from the other Manifestations. Not only does each Manifestation differ in physical features, personality, psychology, but also in the Mission that He must complete. Additionally, each Manifestation has a predestined Revelation to deliver as part of God's Great Plan for Man. Bahá'u'lláh clearly states it when He says that:

"...each Manifestation of God hath a distinct individuality, a definitely prescribed mission, a predestined revelation, and specially designated limitations. Each one of them is known by a different name, is characterized by a special attribute, fulfils a definite mission, and is entrusted with a particular Revelation". (13)

Suffices to recall Abraham's role as the most sublime example of absolute faith in the One and only God Who asks him to sacrifice his son, Isaac, even though God had promised Abraham that his descendants will be as numerous as the stars.

Incapable of understanding why God had asked him to carry out such a deed, Abraham, nevertheless, demonstrates how, an unconditional Faith in an All-knowing and All-Powerful God, resolves the profound doubts we may have about something that God request we do, even if it appears to have no logic or to negate love toward others. (Gen. 22: 1-2)

In the Exodus narrative of the Bible, God gives Moses a specific Mission: to liberate the oppressed Israelites in Egypt from the despotic and unbending rule of the Pharaoh. Moses initially feels incompetent to carry out the task. He presents God his inability to undertake such a task being that He is barely able to express himself verbally, **"O Lord... I am slow of speech and tongue."** (Exo. 4:10) Yet, God reassures Moses that He will talk though him, "...**go I shall help you speak and instruct you what to say**". (Exo. 4:12) After the extraordinary, magnificent, and miraculous crossing of the Red Sea followed by the destruction of the Pharaoh's army (Exo. 14: 15-31), Moses becomes the bearer and presenter of the ten commandments, the Magna Charta of Man's moral behavior towards God and all others (Exo. 20: 1-17). Later, Moses gradually elaborates the many laws for daily living that earned Him the title of the 'Great Legislator' (Exo. Chaps. 21-23).

Buddha had quite a different Mission to fulfill. After his illumination under the Bodhi tree, many sought Him out as Teacher. He revealed to them that life's suffering is brought on by our many unsatisfied desires. The anxiety and pain that we experience are due to our unfulfilled or unattained desires. The key to overcoming the enslavement of pain and suffering is to eliminate all that do not bring us peace or happiness. Therefore, the road to liberation consists in detachment from all that we wish for and do not have. This road to liberation will lead to internal peace, allowing the individual to reach a state of Nirvana, absolute peace, fully liberated from all the material ties that create anguish, desire, and frustration. The inner path of detachment allows the individual to become free of any ties that will impede him to merge with the One and All. As expressed in His teachings, "...**of the spiritual reality** that could be called God; His material expression would be the Universe. Human beings come from that Great Being and go back to Him losing their individuality that separates us from Him as drops of water become one with the ocean" (14). Thus, Buddha becomes the utmost Master of self-renunciation, undertaken to achieve personal liberation or the arrival at Nirvana.

Christ is in charge of showing the Jews (later His followers in pagan lands) the novel trait by which we can call God, "Father": **"Then Jesus lifted his eyes and said, 'Father I give you thanks for having listened to me'..."** (Jn. 11: 41). The filial devotion by which Jesus addresses God is of a magnitude never seen before or deemed possible. Until then, God was mostly perceived as a stern, demanding, and law enforcing Judge. Jesus presented the Jews an unsuspected, tender side of God; that of forgiveness without recrimination, vengeance, or punishment. This new facet was well-described in the parable of the prodigal son, who after prematurely demanded his inheritance from his father, misspent it drinking and whoring, then is joyfully forgiven by his father upon listening to his sincere words of repentance, '**Father I have sinned against heaven and you. I do not deserve to be called your son**'. (Lc. 15: 11-32). This new facet of the Essence of God is so novel, so difficult to assimilate, that even today there are Christians who rather preach a wrathful and judgmental God, more often willing to punish, rather than embracing and forgiving the sinner.

Mohammed was tasked with the Mission of creating a nation obedient to God, from a handful of warring tribes living in the Arabian Peninsula, whose way of life was robbing caravans and enslaving the defeated. From this state of savagery, Mohammed guided these tribes to show and give respect to the conquered, not making them slaves. This was utterly inconceivable prior to the appearance of the Prophet. He was a permanent example of mercy towards all enemies, quality that He instilled on all his followers. It must be pointed out that all the Suras of the Koran, with the exception of one, begin quoting God's Mercy as a most salient of His attributes: **"In the name of Allah, most gracious and most merciful."**

Therefore, the Manifestation is the beacon that allows us to see what God's will is for those to which the Revelation is given. The specific Revelation that the Manifestation delivers becomes the guide, the new course, to be followed by those receiving it in order to grow spiritually and materially.

Duration of the Manifestation's cycle

Upon studying the chronology of the appearance of these extraordinary beings, one can easily detect a pattern in the length of time between one Manifestation and the next--- usually between 500 and 1000 years---both numbers highly symbolic in all Revelations. For example, one can observe that in Christianity, when these years approach, everywhere "millennium" groups appear proclaiming the second coming of Christ.

Seeing this continuity, this systematic appearance of Manifestations throughout the history of mankind, we can affirm that God has, therefore, been continuously present as long as Man has inhabited the earth. Bahá'u'lláh has made note of this reality in the following terms:

> **"His creation hath ever existed, and the Manifestations of His Divine glory and the Day Springs of eternal holiness have been sent down from time immemorial, and been commissioned to summon mankind to the one true God".** (15)

Unfortunately, the existing documentation about the ancient appearance of the innumerable Manifestations is scarce, imprecise and subject to myths and legends that can obscure the truth of who were the Manifestations and what they revealed to those human groups they addressed. What best approximates to being an oral, untainted, but not written

Revelation of a Manifestation of God, are the oral traditions of the Great Spirit of the native tribes of the United States. God is named as the 'Waka Tanka' (or Great Mystery) by the Sioux or 'Gitchi Manitou' by the Algonquians, which is the equivalent of the Great Creator. The Lakota consider him so close to the people, that they called him, 'the Grandfather.' The Blackfoot tribe called him 'Old Man' and declared that He, personally, created everything and taught the Blackfoot how to gain spiritual wisdom in their daily lives. He is referred to as the 'Prime Mover', and His teachings, rather than being a list of goals to attain, are a codicil for daily living. The Chickasaw named Him 'Ababinili', and, according to their beliefs, He is the Creator of all and instructed the Chickasaw how to 'live a long and healthy life.' (16)

In these images we can appreciate the belief of a divine Creator refer to as the 'Great Spirit', which according to their oral traditions became visible at a point in time of their history and taught these indigenous tribes about spirituality and how to lead a better life (moral behaviors included). As we have determined, these are qualities that identify the Manifestations. Based on these scarce evidences we can suspect that these personages were Manifestations of God that appeared to these various tribes, at different moments of their history, essentially teaching them about God and proposing them a spiritual way of life.

Even though we only have skimpy evidences that these Manifestations have been present among mankind since the beginning of time, we do have serious documentation about the most well-known religions established upon the teachings of Krishna, Moses, Zoroaster, Buddha, Jesus Mohammed, and Bahá'u'lláh. It is even more comforting to learn, via the most recent Manifestation, Bahá'u'lláh, that this holy presence of the Manifestations will continue as long as man inhabits this or any other planet:

"These Mirrors will everlastingly succeed each other, and will continue to reflect the light of the Ancient of Days. They that reflect

their glory will, in like manner, continue to exist for evermore, for the Grace of God can never cease from flowing. This is a truth that none can disprove". (17)

It could not be otherwise. God who has created man to His 'image and likeness' would not leave his most precious creation abandoned without any guidance as to what is his goal in life, his role in Creation. Without that guidance he would not be able to develop to his full potential, that of becoming aware that his role in life is to continue evolution developing through his creativity, and to become a brilliant testimonial of God's presence in his soul through his material, moral, and spiritual achievements.

We will call "Progressive Revelation" to God's continuous presence in the history of mankind and we will examine it in detail in the following chapter.

Chapter 4
References

1) Bahá'u'lláh, The Kitáb-i-Íqán, p. 178
2) Bahá'u'lláh, Gleanings from the Writings of Bahá'u'lláh, XXIX. p. 70
3) Bahá'u'lláh, Gleanings from the Writings of Bahá'u'lláh", XXXIV p. 79
4) Bahá'u'lláh, The Kitáb-i-Íqán, p. 154
5) Sura 3, 59
6) Bahá'u'lláh, The Kitáb-i-Íqán, p. 20
7) Bahá'u'lláh, The Kitáb-i-Íqán, p. 153
8) Bahá'u'lláh, Gleanings from the Writings of Bahá'u'lláh, XXXIV p. 79
9) Example of the many historians that have made such affirmations and have given enough documentation to back it up- Centralized/decentralized economies - Primitive to Slavery
Content copyright: Nathan Davis 2003-2013

Centralized/decentralized economies - Primitive to Slavery www.after-capitalism.com/society-after-capitalism/economies_ps.html

How Slavery Helped Build a World Economy. *Excerpted from* Jubilee: the Emergence of African-American Culture *by the Schomburg Center for Research in Black Culture* - How Slavery Helped Build a World Economy news.nationalgeographic.com/news/2003/.../0131_030203_jubilee2_2.ht

Slavery from Roman Times to the Early Transatlantic Trade -books.google.com.bz/books?isbn=0719018250 William D. Phillips - 1985

10) Google. Civil War US. Encyclopedia Wikipedia. *wikipedia.org/wiki/American_Civil_War*

11) Google. Slavery in Brazil. _slavery in Brazil_ - historic clothing _histclo.com/act/work/slave/am/sa-bra.htm_

12) Bahá'u'lláh, The Kitáb-i-Aqdás, paragraph 72 p. 45

13) Bahá'u'lláh, Gleanings from the Writings of Bahá'u'lláh, XXII, p. 51

14) José Luis Marqués, Educadores de la Humanidad, pg. 90

15) Bahá'u'lláh, Gleanings from the Writings of Bahá'u'lláh, LXXXVII, p. 173

16) Google. The Great Spirit. Encyclopedia Wikipedia, _wikipedia.org/wiki/Great_Spirit_

17) Bahá'u'lláh, Gleanings from the Writings of Bahá'u'lláh, XXX, p. 73

Chapter 5

Progressive Revelation

How to understand Progressive Revelation?

Why progressive? Because man evolves gradually. In the course of his evolution, he apprehends objective reality, understands the intimacy of the physical world, captures the essence of his being, discovers his respectful relationship to nature and to others, identifies his role in the cosmos. All of these advances have a corresponding evolutionary spiritual stage.

Man also experiences Life as a natural cycle (infancy, childhood, youth, adulthood, senior age) much the same way that Nature has its own cycle (spring, summer, autumn, winter). If all reality evolves through its natural cycles, why can't God's Revelation have its own cycle of birth, growth, splendor, and finality? In fact, Revelation has its own "natural cycle" which is adapted to the level of spiritual maturity that people have when it is given to them.

This is precisely how Bahá'u'lláh addresses the appearance of a Revelation. He places it within the context of a natural growth cycle based on man's tempo of internal growth. One of the many ways He describes such process is a follows:

"And now concerning thy question regarding the nature of religion. Know thou that they who are truly wise have likened the world unto the human temple. As the body of man needeth a garment to clothe it, so the body of mankind must needs be adorned with the mantle of justice and wisdom. Its robe is the Revelation vouchsafed unto it by God. Whenever this robe hath fulfilled its purpose, the Almighty will assuredly renew it". (1)

From the above explanation, we can assume that Revelation appears continuously throughout the history of mankind, but that its content is given according to the capacity for understanding of its recipients, and the state of spiritual, intellectual, and material evolution of the people receiving it. This is how Bahá'u'lláh explains this idea:

"For every age requireth a fresh measure of the light of God. Every Divine Revelation hath been sent down in a manner that befitted the circumstances of the age in which it hath appeared". (2)

This means that each Revelation is not final, that its contents can be presented in a higher level of comprehension. Revelation is not given **once and forever**, precluding a subsequent Revelation from appearing. Divine Revelation is relative in its content because it is adapted to the capacity of the listeners at the time of its disclosure. Therefore, a new Revelation is open to new interpretations, deeper meanings, and new levels of comprehension.

Stated in another way, because each Revelation is not definitive and close, it is, therefore, **subordinate** to the new Revelation and the new changes it may bring. These changes and these differences are especially evident with regards to individual and social behavioral practices, rather than to the content of Who God is. Social norms are more susceptible to change because they are continuously modified according to the pace of mankind's cultural, technical, and intellectual evolution, normally faster in change than his spirituality.

What is most impacted when a new Revelation arrives and offers a new perspective on beliefs that until then were considered fixed and immovable? The dogmas established by priests, religious leaders, ministers, pastors, and mullahs are most affected. These dogmas are presented as the official and only valid interpretation of the Revelation received. The dogmas attempt to make clear those aspects or details of the Revelation that do not appear to be that transparent or easy to understand, such as the dogma of the Trinity in Christianity. According to the religious leaders, these dogmas cannot be questioned or revised. Once established, these dogmas are to be accepted and defended by their followers in order to be acknowledged as members of that religious community. Yet, in the context of Progressive Revelation, such dogmas can be revised, even abolished. This can happen when the next Revelation clarifies aspects of the previous Revelation that were misinterpreted or not understood at all. When this happens then some of the dogmas can be revised, or even abolished. Such was the case of the dogmatic believe that the Jewish priests had developed that the Messiah would come and establish a powerful earthly kingdom liberating them from the Roman oppression. Jesus rectified such dogmatic belief by defining His Kingdom as the Kingdom of the Spirit (Heaven), not the expected earthly kingdom. (Mathew 5: 3 – John 18: 36) This was precisely what the priests accused Jesus before the Roman governor, that He had proclaimed to be King, and therefore He should be put to death.

Only God can change His Revelation, clarify it, enhance it, or modify it, according to His view on how well prepared its listeners are to enter their next stage of spiritual evolution. God can and does make those changes through His revealed Word presented by His Manifestation. The unique nature of the Manifestation is to be God's Spokesperson as we explained in Chapter 3. The authority to effect the change comes from God but the Manifestation is the one that makes the change visible, audible, and known to those He gives the new Revelation.

Generally, the majority of people are born, raised, and socialized within a Revelation they firmly believe in. Hearing something different other than the Revelation learned since infancy requires an open heart and mind because, surely, what the new Manifestation proposes will be at a higher level of knowledge and understanding of God, a different spiritual relationship with Him, and others. When the Manifestation reveals changes to the dogmas, beliefs and truths on which a person's faith is based, that individual is forced to view those dogmas in a different perspective, under a different optic. This implies he must modify his beliefs based on the certainty and confidence that what the most recent Manifestation has revealed is the vision and perspective that God wants him to have now.

This gradual disclosure of Revelation that God offers man is His recognition that humanity has a slow spiritual growth. It is called 'Progressive Revelation' because each new Revelation utilizes new concepts that are more profound, richer in meaning and in revealing Who God is, as well as letting us know how best we can achieve a personal and collective relationship with Him. It is the gradual manner by which God has revealed Himself to humanity.

God directs the spiritual, intellectual, and even material evolution of man

We have stated that God, since the beginning of man on Earth, has been there directing his evolution, especially his spiritual development, although it seems that man has made little progress in this area due to the astonishing atrocities he continues to inflict on his relatives, neighbors and enemies. The daily level of violence, hate, persecution and exploitation is such that we can easily agree with the philosophical maxim, *"the fiercest predator man has to face is other men."* *

---

* 'Analysis of this topic done in great detail by Pareja in *Sisyphus, the Evolutionary Infancy of Humanity.*]

Keeping in mind that this is historically true, we cannot deny the modest progress man has made with regards to his spirituality, human relations, ethics, and morality. Let's recall several of the most well known improvements. As God has decreed, we have ceased to have bloody animal sacrifices. The custom of older civilizations of sacrificing boys, girls, and virgins to satisfy the supposed demands of their gods has been abolished. Currently, at both the international and legal level, we do not accept the concept of slavery---once a common and ordinary means of dealing with men and women captured during wars and conflicts by selling them to the highest bidder as if they were cattle at an animal fair.

We have stopped persecuting men and women accused of witchcraft or heresy, condemning them to torture and death simply because they questioned, with sound reasoning, the content of a dogma established and imposed by the Church. In some cases these 'heretics' were simply mentally unstable individuals who were wrongly diagnosed. We have managed to reach an agreement among 130 nations whereby we have the defined the rights of all men, women and children based on the fact they are either man, woman or child. We have crafted international laws that specify the acceptable treatment of prisoners of war. An international court of justice has been established to prosecute those accused of crimes against humanity. There are national and international proposals that regulate the use of pesticides and other chemicals in order to prevent environmental contamination. Use of atomic weapons in military conflict has been restrained. Today it is considered inappropriate in the US to use the word 'nigger' to refer to African-American descendents from the slaves brought over from Africa. There is also a worldwide conversation regarding women's equal rights to those of men that were historically denied to half of humanity for thousands of years.

Despite this significant list of man's evolutionary spiritual advances, we can argue that in various parts of the world there are too many examples of persons or groups of individuals who continue to infringe on the ethical and moral principles, which should be guiding their behavior. Although this may be true, it cannot be denied that humanity has improved its ethical/ moral conduct when we compare ancient behaviors that today are unacceptable, yet in those ancient times were not only considered "normal," but were practiced by the majority of countries without sanctions.

These advancements have not come free of charge, nor are they due solely to man's spontaneous enlightenment. A large number of them are the result of a Revelation made by God, through his envoy, His Manifestation, who, upon appearing, delivers to the people the new plan God has for them, including the role they are expected to play in mankind's evolution. The task normally is expressed via a pact made by the Manifestation, in the name of God, with the people to whom He speaks. This agreement is expressed in several books of the Bible as a covenant[2], such as in Deuteronomy:

"Know therefore that the LORD thy God, he
***is* God, the faithful God, which keepeth the**

---

[2]   The term 'covenant' appears 280 times in the King James Version of the bible with different meanings. Foremost in the Old Testament it was a solemn agreement which served the function of a written contract. The term was also used to refer to an agreement made between a stronger foe, or a victor with its conquered (Gen 14:13). Covenant was also used as a promise to respect boundaries (Gen 31:44). The most important meaning was the relationship of God with mankind. God made a covenant with Noah promising not to destroy mankind with a deluge again (Gen. 9:11) and on mount Sinai, God made a covenant designating Israel as His people and declaring Himself as their only God (Ex. 19:11 ff- Jer 7:23 – Ezk 11:20). There are other meanings of covenant not included here because they are not pertinent to the pact of God and his people. (John McKenzie, *Dictionary of the Bible*, pg.153-157) The Baha'i Faith's use of the word refers explicitly to the designation of Bahá'u'lláh's son, Abdu'l-Bahá, as the Center of the Covenant, in charge of maintaining the unity of the Faith. Before passing away Bahá'u'lláh left a written Will and Testament in which He appointed His son to be the sole interpreter of His Writings, thus preventing any sects or denominations from springing up and dividing the unity of His Revelation.

covenant and mercy with them that love him and keep his commandments to a thousand generations;" (Deuteronomy 7:9)

And in Leviticus:

And I will walk among you, and will be your God, and ye shall be my people. (Leviticus 26:12)

The pact assures, from God, His divine assistance, His infallible presence in the life of the individual as well as in the lives of the members of the group addressed by the Manifestation. God keeps His promise regardless of how often man breaks it. As far as man is concerned, the agreement requires that he acknowledges God as the only God, above whom there is no other god, and, subsequently, to live according to the divine, ethical, moral and social precepts introduced by the Manifestation. This is well expressed in Exodus:

"Now therefore, if ye will obey my voice indeed, and keep my Covenant, then ye shall be a peculiar treasure unto me above all people." (Exodus 19:5)

When the Manifestation presents the pact that God wants to make with them, He does so at God's direct representative, but, at the same time, as the Master, the Guide and the divine Healer of the particular group of people He addresses at that particular moment in history. Both the guidance and the medicine are provided by the revealed divine precepts and by the inspiration that the Manifestation can convey to its followers, reviving their awareness of God, fine tuning their perception of the role that God plays in their daily lives, pointing out how to live in harmony with God and the needs of his brother and his fellow men.

God promises permanent assistance and a glorious evolution of the people He has addressed as long as they remain faithful to the divine pact. The aid is evidenced in the multiple practical inventions that seem to sprout within the group addressed by the Manifestation. Innovations appear profusely in many areas such as architecture, engineering, and agriculture. For example, the discovery of meat dehydration allowed whole groups of people to preserve meat for days or months without spoiling giving them a chance to conserve food while traveling or waiting for the next hunt to take place; improved philosophical reasoning unraveled existential truths that have always haunted mankind; renewed artistic efforts have led to the creation of marvelous works of art; an explosion of new songs, poetry and literature have enriched the culture of the people where the Manifestation has appeared. The net result of the acceptance and putting into practice of the agreement as presented by the Manifestation has been the development of an extraordinary civilization that stands out in historic annals, leaving plain evidence of their growth. This growth spurt has occurred despite the flaws of the followers who may not have upheld the pact proposed by the Manifestation.

Examples of Progressive Revelation

Let's look at some concrete examples of how Progressive Revelation occurred when the new Manifestation repealed, changed, or modified a moral or ethical law of the previous Revelation.

Before going into details, it is necessary to clarify a key point: God's mandates in the corresponding Revelation are quite straightforward and brief. Yet, their application is not that simple. Life's circumstances are numerous, varied, unpredictable, changing. The moral or ethical principle almost always has required that the mandate be translated and adapted to particular cases or situations. This normally has occurred when individuals have presented specific problems or when unforeseeable events have demanded religious leaders for a concrete solution. From these situations, or from hypothetical questions about specific cases, large compendiums are made instructing inquirers how to put into practice the revealed principles.

Perhaps the best place to begin is the Ten Commandments, presented by Moses as coming directly from God. They will allow us to understand how subsequent Manifestations modified their application, without changing the essential guidelines.

Worshipping the only one God

If there is one commandment that has remained the same throughout all the Manifestations, it is the recognition that God is only One. It is the foundation, the basis, and the axis, on which all Revelations rest and have their reason for being. The categorical, unequivocal affirmations that there is only one God, that there are no other gods above Him, beside Him or beneath Him, is the affirmation without which no other principles of any Revelation have validity. It is the **uniqueness, the absolute and total independence** from any other divinity that gives God the supreme authority to give man a Life Plan. He wishes to do that because man is God's most remarkable and marvelous creation. The Plan is designed for man's improvement, for his internal growth, for the fulfillment of the end for which he was created. For this reason the Manifestation appears, to explain the Plan.

Worshipping God, acknowledging His Supremacy as Creator of all that is, especially us who are created in "his own image and likeness", is essential to the recognition that He is the One God above Whom there is no other god. A necessary step is to find the best word that identifies such a Being. What is the most accurate and appropriate name to represent Him? What word most adequately describes, without ambiguities, that God is God, that there is no other god above Him?

To find the most appropriate word in their own language to name the Creator has been a genuine effort among those dedicated to understanding this nameless Being. The Hebrews, for example, considered inadmissible that the Almighty, the Unknowable God should have a name and thus He was referred to only by the letters JHWH. Others have sought earnestly for the word or words, in their language, that can best express who

God is. Thus, in English we have 'God'; in German, 'Gott'; in Latin, 'Deus'; in Italian, 'Dio'; in French, 'Dieu'; in Portuguese, 'Deus'; in Greek, 'Theos'; in Catalan, 'Déu'; in Farsi, 'Ahura Mazda' (Supreme God); in Hebrew: 'JHWH', 'El', 'Elohim', 'El-Shaddai', and 'Emmanuel'. In Arabic, 'Allah' (although the Hadiths state that Mohammed gave God 99 names (attributes of God). Whatever word has been chosen, the important thing is to accept the relativity of a language to give God the best name that communicates the reality that He is the Only God, Creator of all that is, the same God of all revealed religions. And the best worship given to God is using the chosen word to name Him within the context of prayer and the rituals whose finality is to acknowledge God as the Only God.

Burnt Offerings

The first mandate given by God to recognize Him as God is clearly stated in the Ten Commandments. Nevertheless, it existed in Adam's time when his sons, Cain and Abel, in adoration and recognition of God as Creator, made an offering to Him using fruits of their labor. Cain made a gift of the fruits from the earth he had tilled; Abel offered the first-born of his herd. Both offerings were sacrificed and burned as an oblation of adoration to God (Gen. 4: 1-5). Later on, Abraham converts this same sacrifice into the ultimate symbolic act of a man whose faith in one God takes him to the brink of sacrificing his own son. God stops him from doing only after Abraham has proven his absolute obedience. So, instead of sacrificing his son, Isaac, Abraham offers to sacrifice a sheep that has become tangled in a thorn bush. (Gen. 22: 15-17) The establishment of burnt sacrifices as a mean of adoring and praising God make sense in so much that a live animal represents Life. The innocent animal depends solely on his master who decides how long it will live. At the moment it is selected for sacrifice, it will no longer live or reproduce. Sacrificing a life in honor of God is man's symbolic gesture of unconditional acknowledgment that God is the Creator of Life; that Life belongs to Him and to Him it is returned.

After the receipt of the Ten Commandments, Aaron, Moses' brother, is ordained by God as the high priest. The priesthood is then established and the priests become responsible for developing a whole set of detailed rituals specifying how sacrifices were to be conducted in order to express the various relationships of man to God. The main reason was to acknowledge that Yahweh is the God of Israel to Whom adoration and devotion are due (Exo. 20: 22-24). But, the burnt offering expressed many other things depending on how it was carried out such as representing a symbolic devotion to Yahweh (Exo. 29:18); or it could express the consecration of the ritual covenant at Mount Sinai (Exo. 24: 5) or the celebration of a personal covenant, such as the one that God did with Jacob (Gen. 31: 44). The offerings were used for the consecration of priests (Lv. 9), for the consecration of the Temple (Kings 8: 64), and the celebration of the Ark being brought to Jerusalem (2 Sam. 10:17). The burnt offerings also expressed the release from sin (Exo. 29: 14, 36); or were used for the purification after the birth of a child (Lv. 12: 6), and as a token of thankfulness (Psal. 50:14). In addition, there were sacrifices of animal parts, which took place for specific reasons, such an offering to celebrate a victory (1 Sam.11: 15).

When Jesus appeared on the scene, at least 1,500 years had passed during which sacrifices in the name of God were essential to the covenant between God and His people. The burnt sacrifice represented the backbone of this relationship. There is not one solemn occasion in which burnt sacrifices were not part of the celebration. Priests made their livelihood from them. So did the merchants who prepared the animals for sale at the Temple of Jerusalem; thus, their indignation when Jesus overturned their tables inside the Temple (Mt. 21: 12-13).

The overthrowing of the merchants tables in the Temple of Jerusalem was Jesus direct challenge to the priests, as well as the symbolic abolishment of such burnt sacrifices as the medium to declare ritually God's Majesty and Sovereignty. After Jesus death on the cross as the Sacrificial Lamb, the long

---

history of bloody sacrifices introduced by Moses' Revelation quickly disappears.

How to Pray to God

Jesus also radically changed the way in which man can pray to God. He repeals the inveterate expression of public adoration based on genuflections, arm waving, using specific garments, and making loud recitals. Jesus replaces this ritualistic way of praying with a new form of worship, done in the intimacy of one's chamber, from one's own heart to the Father:

> **"And when you pray, do not imitate the hypocrites: they love to say their prayers standing up in the synagogues and at the street corners for people to see them... when you pray, go to your private room, shut yourself in, and so pray to your Father who is in that secret place ...So you should pray like this: Our Father in heaven,"** (Mt. 6, 5-9)

This novel way of conversation with God can be done by anyone, in private, without having to explicitly go to a site designated by the priests for that purpose. In comparison to the tradition of public prayer ongoing for hundreds and hundreds of years, this is an extraordinary change in the format of worship.

When Mohammed appears in Arabia, animal sacrifices, common in Judaism, are relegated to only one holiday. Besides this, there is never mention again of animal sacrifice as a means by which God expects to be praised. It is replaced with obligatory prayers that all Moslems must recite five times a day, kneeling and touching their foreheads to the ground. By instructing them in this manner, Mohammed replicates the dramatic change of worship of God instituted by Jesus.

No killing

In the annals of ancient history, homicide is rampant. There is no civilization that has not left recorded in its history the deeds of its heroes, battling, and killing the "enemy". The annihilation of the supposed "enemy" is motive for national celebration recorded in songs, poems, paintings, dances, stories and books. These records are mostly about the group, the tribe, the nation; but, at the individual level, it was common to write about a confrontation between two foes, only one emerging victorious. Typical of this scenario is the face-off between Achilles and Hector prior to the siege of Troy.

The precept "thou shall not kill" has existed historically in varying forms, in all religions, regardless of how man has persistently killed his fellow beings all along his presence on Earth. Let us review the major religious expressions of this moral law:

- Hinduism's most ancient writings, the Vedas, clearly address the principle of non-violence (Ahims), extending it to animals. The Vedas state: **"to hurt sentient beings hampers the reception of celestial blessings… the murderer of animals is incapable of tasting the message of Absolute Truth"**. (3)
- Moses specified it in four plain words, **"Thou shall not kill"** (Exo. 20: 13) but afterwards had to detail the circumstances by which killing was acceptable. He also instituted the rule by which one could claim the same level of damage received: **"If further harm is done, however, you will award life for life, eye for eye, tooth for tooth, hand for hand, foot for foot, burn for burn, wound for wound, stroke for stroke"** (Exo. 21: 23-25).
- Another law clarified what should be done if **"anyone has struck his fellow accidentally, without any previous feud with him"** (Deut. 19, 4).The Book of Numbers specified that anyone accused of murder could not be put to death without a trial, and **"the community will decide in accordance with these rules between**

the one who struck the blow and the avenger of blood". (Num. 35: 24)

- Zoroaster did not use words/concepts as explicit as Moses', but the substance of the commandment remained the same when he said: **"Furor is to be rejected! Avoid violence you who wish to assure yourselves with the reward of the Good Doctrine whose companion is the saintly man. He will have his dwelling in your mansion, Lord".** (4) Here is a clear allusion to avoiding violence whose worst expression is causing the death of another.

- Buddha took the roots of Hinduism's "do not kill" mandate under which He was born and used it in context of moral behavior of an individual whose life is governed by five ethical principles, first of which is respect for human life. This, in turn, implies not taking it away from any living creature, human or animal. This rule does not exclude self-defense. (5)

- Jesus further refined the concept of **"Thou shall not kill…"** by affirming, **"But I say this to you, anyone who is angry with a brother will answer for it before the court;…".** (Mt. 5: 22) And if this were not revolutionary enough, He pushed the concept further when stating that one must love his enemy, **""You have heard how it was said, You will love your neighbor and hate your enemy. But I say this to you, 'love your enemies and pray for those who persecute you; so that you may be children of your Father in heaven"** (Mt.5, 43-45).

- Mohammed expressed this law in terms similar to those of Moses, because, due to level of aggression between Arab tribes, the least He could do was to give them a clear mandate for control, **"And do not kill any one whom Allah has forbidden, except for a just cause, and whoever is slain unjustly, We have indeed given authority to his next of kin, so let him not exceed the just limits in slaying; surely he is aided".** (6)

- Although Bahá'u'lláh, in his book of laws, the *Kitáb-i-Aqdás*, sanctions the mandate **"not to kill,"** (7), He nevertheless exhorts His followers to the higher standard of **"rather than kill is its better to die in the path of God's will"** (8)

Not to initiate war

A precept that complements the "do not kill" mandate addresses the act of starting a war. Although not an explicit commandment, it is certainly a recommendation that intensifies with each Manifestation until it becomes fully explicit with Mohammed. Mohammed transformed the act of premeditated aggression to acquire territory in order to gain natural resources or personal wealth into the concept of non-violence. The use of arms is only acceptable to God when one is under attack, which implies, solely for self-defense.

During the time of Krishna and Moses, war was the most common and acceptable, almost natural practice by which disputes, land grabs, and punishment to the 'enemies of God' were carried out. Several examples attest to that fact. The Bhagavad-Gita (The Song of the Lord) is most well -known book about Hinduism in the West. It is a dialogue between Arjuna (his first disciple) and Krishna (The Supreme Personality of Godhead) about transcendent aspects of life, about knowledge of God, nature, time and activity (karma). What is truly noteworthy of the dialogue between Arjuna and Krishna is that it takes place precisely when Arjuna prepares for battle against an army of Dhristarahstra's relatives encamped at Kuruksetra. (9) It sounds contradictory that a Revelation about the meaning of Life and God is given on a battlefield. Yet, at the same time, it is symbolic, since Life itself is a battle in which each one must fight in order to overcome oneself in order to find out the meaning of his own existence and his relationship to God.

During Moses' time, the Israelites engaged in many battles for possession of the Promised Land. Many of them involved the presence and leadership of Moses, as was the case of the battle against Amalek, in which Moses had to continuously keep his arms raised in order for the Israelites to win (Exo. 17: 8-13). In another occasion, Moses orders each tribe to select one thousand men to form the army necessary to go to war against Midian (Num. 31:6).

Yahweh, who ensures that the Israelites become an autonomous nation, He does so by endorsing many of the battles carried out by His people. The Israelites, in turn, credit Him for their victories (Exo. 14: 14; - Deut. 1: 30, 32, 41;- Jos. 2: 24; 10:14; 42: 23,10; - Judges 5: 23). The decision to go to war is not arbitrary; it is made within the scope of God's Will, as interpreted by Moses or Aaron.

Buddha never participated in any religious battle, much less in conquest. His respect for Life in general made Him the supreme pacifist. His followers, Buddhist monks of Tibet and, especially China, had to develop an art of self-defense (possibly the origin of Kung Fu and the martial arts) when they were shamelessly attacked by common thieves as they begged for food or when their monasteries were razed arbitrarily by soldiers of the tribal or regional chief. In His teachings regarding Life, even that of animals, there is no room for warfare, and less so for the reasons which he had pointed out as the causes of suffering and which, simultaneously, were the motives for war: desire for land, ownership of natural wealth, confiscation of sumptuous buildings, jewels laden with precious stones, utensils made from silver and gold, possession of women (victory trophies) for sexual exploitation and delight.

Jesus remained in line with Buddha's teaching because He did not participate in any organized or violent demonstration against the priests or civil authority, except for the overturning the tables of the money-changers in the Temple, "**Then he went into the Temple and began driving out those who were busy trading, saying to them, 'According to scripture, my house shall be a house of prayer but you have turned it into a bandits' den'**". (Lk. 19: 45-46). Aside from that event, He never led a demonstration against the political rulers, did not organize an armed group, and did not instigate His followers to rebel politically against the priests or the Romans. What He did change, modify or abolish were some sacred traditions the Jews had received from Moses as part of their spiritual inheritance.

Among Jesus new teachings this one clearly stands out: abstaining to respond to violence with more violence stands out, **"But I say this to you: offer no resistance to the wicked. On the contrary, if anyone hits you on the right cheek, offer him the other as well"** (Mt.5: 39).This was ratified when Peter cut off the ear of the servant of the High Priest and Jesus rebuked him, **"Jesus then said, 'Put your sword back, for all who draw the sword will die by the sword".** (Mt. 26: 52) But this was not an act of submission or cowardice, as demonstrated by His reproach of the guard who struck Him while He was being interrogated by Caiphas, the High Priest, **"Jesus replied, 'If there is some offence in what I said, point it out; but if not, why do you strike me?'"** (Jn. 18:23) At no time did Jesus incite his followers to use armed combat as a means of gaining supporters or propagating His Message.

As we have seen, Mohammed lived at a time when the law of retaliation "an eye for an eye" prevailed, aggression, and assault and robbery were part of the daily lives of the nomadic tribes in the Arabian Peninsula. In this context, without the background of extensive and intensive religious teachings of the Jews, the new concept of the Prophet that **"unilateral warfare is not acceptable"** did not exist. Instead, it was fully accepted that the winner of the battle took the spoils, could enslave the defeated, including women and children. Mohammed modifies this cultural belief imposing a new rule: not to take the initiative to attack any tribe with the aim of plundering, making slaves of the defeated. Arms are to be used *only* to defend themselves when attacked or when Islam is threatened:

> **"Fight those who do not believe in Allah, nor in the latter day, nor do they prohibit what Allah and His Apostle have prohibited, nor follow the religion of truth, out of**

those who have been given the Book (Jews and Christians**), until they pay the tax in acknowledgment of superiority and they are in a state of subjection".** (10) [names included for clarification]

It is within this context that we can understand the use of force. Modern day Jihad, associated with terrorist attacks perpetuated by Moslem fanatical groups who view the Western culture and values as enemies of Islam, interprets this as a call to battle. Nevertheless, the original goal of Jihad is to promote self-control. This is the ultimate Jihad. In order to reach it, Muslims must constantly fight the negative tendencies that keep them away from God.

Bahá'u'lláh goes beyond the religious justification for war by inviting His followers to follow His directive of: "**Know ye that to be killed in the path of His good pleasure is better for you than to kill**" (11) This directive should be considered even when faced with persecution. Although one could argue this is a case for self-defense, the governing body of the Baha'I Faith, the Universal House of Justice, proposes total sacrifice, stating "**organized attacks against Baha'is should never lead to warring conflicts, since this is strictly forbidden in our Teachings…**" (12)

This teaching is strictly followed by the Bahá'is of Iran (its largest religious minority---over 300,000) who are constantly persecuted. Since 1979, the Iranian government has not ceased persecuting them, merely for being Bahá'ís, confiscating their belongings, prohibiting their access to universities (or expelling them when identified as such), denying them their rights to retirement, social security and employment; destroying their homes, even their cemeteries. In the year 2011 there were more than 400 arrests, the majority without trial. Inside the Iranian prison many have suffered torture and death. There is documentation of 219 Baha'is who have died for having being steadfast to their religious beliefs in the period 1979-2005. (13)

No stealing

This commandment is similarly brief and explicit in the Ten Commandments bequeathed by God through Moses, "Do not steal" (Gen. 20: 15). Its most extreme form of punishment was death, (Deut. 24: 7); the least extreme punishment was restitution, which implied paying back double of what was stolen, **"If the stolen animal is found alive in his possession, be it ox, donkey or animal from the flock, he will pay back double"** (Ex. 22: 3).

Jesus upheld the "do not steal" Commandment as stated by Moses in the Decalogue. He confirmed that restitution was necessary during his encounter with Zacchaeus, the Jewish tax collector. Tax collectors, working for both the priests and the Romans during the time of Jesus, were hated by the Jews because they shameless stole from all who paid the taxes through them. Jesus asked Zacchaeus to receive Him in his home and when they are dining together, Zacchaeus confesses his sin, stealing the tax money, and promises Jesus, **"Look, sir, I am going to give half my property to the poor, and if I have cheated anybody I will pay him back four times the amount"**. To this confession Jesus praises him, **"Today salvation has come to this house, because this man too is a son of Abraham;"** (Lk. 19: 1-10). With these words, Jesus not only praises and rewards Zacchaeus, but approves of the generous restitution, more than double the amount specified by Moses.

A clear affirmation indicating Mohammed elaborated on the topic of robbery cannot be easily found in the Koran. Stealing is simply included among the acts, which all Moslems should abstain from, as indicated in Sura 60:

> **"O Prophet! when believing women come to you giving you a pledge that they will not associate aught with Allah, and *will not steal*, and will not commit fornication, and will not kill their children, and will not bring a calumny**

which they have forged of themselves, and will not disobey you in what is good, accept their pledge, and ask forgiveness for them from Allah; surely Allah is Forgiving, Merciful". (14)

The Koran is not explicit as to what should be the punishment for theft, except that it should be "painful", **"And their taking usury though indeed they were forbidden it and their devouring the property of people falsely, We have prepared for the unbelievers from among them a painful chastisement".** (15)

Bahá'u'lláh also warns his followers, "d**o not steal**". When unfortunately this does happens Baha'is are bound by the criminal law system of their country of residence.

Matrimony

Civilizations prior to the appearance of Israel have similar beliefs and behaviors with respect to marriage. The more political power and wealth a man had, the more expanded was his "right" to have various wives. In the case of the rulers they had the acquiescence of possessing various women as concubines, the equivalent of sexual servants.

Previous Manifestations were aware of this deeply inherited custom of accepted polygamy. It was extremely difficult to change the custom because the people they spoke to were not ready for such a change and, thus, the Manifestations of those times did not prohibit the lawful marriage to multiple wives. But, as other Manifestations appeared afterwards, God gives men higher standards regarding the control of his sexual urges; taking on responsibility for his sexual contacts outside marriage, especially when they resulted in children out of wedlock, who were normally left unprotected becoming the sole responsibility of the woman.

Let us briefly examine how the institution of marriage to only one woman evolved through the different Manifestations, as man's comprehension of the benefits of monogamy matures. From the beginning of the Bible, the practice of taking concubines appears, as was the case of Reumah, the concubine of Nahor, Abraham's brother (Gen. 22: 23-24). Abraham, for his part, also engages with a concubine. Sarah, his wife, apparently is barren. Conscious of this fact and that Abraham will not have the numerous progeny that God had promised him because of her sterility, Sarah advises Abraham, **"'Listen, now! Since Yahweh has kept me from having children, go to my slave-girl. Perhaps I shall get children through her.' And Abram took Sarai's advice".** (Gen.16: 1-2)

Abraham accepts Sarah's proposal and beds Hagar, the slave, without her consent, because as a slave she had no rights, and could not reject or decline the wishes of her master. From this sexual encounter, the boy Ishmael is born. Sarah initially accepts Ishmael as Abraham's son.

When many years later Sarah conceives Isaac, the arrangement no longer works. Sarah does not accept that Ishmael should inherit the rights of the first born because Ishmael is not her own child. For this reason, she asks Abraham to banish Hagar with Ishmael. Initially Abraham refuses to do so, but later accepts upon receiving a message from Yahweh's instructing to carry out Sarah's wishes while assuring Abraham that Ishmael, as well, will be the father of numerous descendants (Gen. 21: 9-14). This is an excellent example of how difficult it is to maintain a conjugal relationship with two women concurrently, under the same roof, trying to treat them equally.

Years later, Moses liberates the Israelites from enslavement in Egypt and subsequently receives the Ten Commandments from Yahweh. One of the commandments clearly forbids sexual relations outside the marriage by stating, **"thou shall not commit adultery"** (Ex. 20: 14) and the last clearly stipulates that adultery cannot be committed with the wife of a fellow man: **"thou shall not covet thy neighbor's wife"** (Exo. 20: 17).

This does not prevent the sons of the chosen people from taking on concubines as normal practice. Such was the case of Samuel, who had a concubine named Rizpah (2 Sam. 3: 7), and whom Abner, his military ally, also beds (2 Sam 3: 7).

When David was being pursued by Absalom and fled Jerusalem, he left behind ten concubines taking care of his home (2 Sam 15: 16). Roboam, son of Solomon, had eighteen wives and sixty concubines (2 Cron. 11: 21). According to the Song of Songs, Solomon, at the height of his glory, had "**sixty queens, and eighty concubines**" (Song of Songs 6: 8)

Jesus accepts this commandment given to Moses and elevates it to a higher level of purity when He proposes: **"But I say this to you, if a man looks at a woman lustfully, he has already committed adultery with her in his heart"**. (Mt. 5: 28). This new heightened perspective - merely having lustful thoughts about a woman are equivalent to committing adultery with her -- certainly requires a degree of spiritual fortitude not previously addressed by prior Manifestations. Based on these instructions and affirmations, Christianity decrees that a man should only have one wife in marriage.

The situation that Mohammad encounters among the Arabs is one of continuous fighting among nomadic dessert tribes looking to snatch merchandise and riches from others as a 'normal way of life'. During these battles, men died frequently, leaving women and girls completely unprotected and open to abuse. Mohammad, wishing to protect those women who became widows upon the death of their husbands in battle, married five of them. He did so to show how widows should be protected and treated equally when taken into marriage. Nevertheless, in the Koran He left clear instructions restricting the number of wives to a maximum of four, and, in that case, under a condition very difficult to meet:

> **"And if you fear that you cannot act equitably towards orphans, then marry such women as seem good to you, two and three and four;**

but if you fear that you will not do justice (between them), then (marry) only one or what your right hands possess; this is more proper, that you may not deviate from the right course". (16)

The phrase **"but if you fear that you will not do justice (between them)"** refers to equal treatment that must be given to each wife, that is, equal status, treatment and comfort. If such treatment is obviously not forthcoming, then the directive of only one wife is equally clear. This new orientation, compared to the way the Israelites were openly living with their concubines, is a significant development. Equally revolutionary is Mohammad's directive ordering a husband to give a dowry to his bride, dowry that she can use at will and that remains solely hers, even upon the death of the husband. Until then, it was customary for the family of the male to keep the dowry, especially among Jews. In case of divorce, according to Mohammad, the husband is not to take anything he has given her (understood that it refers to any material possessions). Furthermore, Mohammad, specifies that on a divorce the man is to compensate the woman with "a fair compensation". (17) When the new rights for women decreed by Mohammad are analyzed in the context of the period in which they were given, they are quite extraordinary given that during this time women had no rights, infanticide of female babies was acceptable, and women were basically items of property to be used by man as he wished.

Bahá'u'lláh endorses the monogamy proposed by Christianity and presents it as God's Will when He affirms:

"Whoso contenteth himself with a single partner from among the maidservants of God, both he and she shall live in tranquility". (18)

Additionally, Bahá'u'lláh gives marriage to only one woman a very high role within God's Plan. Parents have to become aware of the magnificent gift of procreation that they have been endowed with. This gift entails that their children will one day participate in the choir of those that Bless God for their existence. This is how Bahá'u'lláh expresses it:

"Enter into wedlock, O people, that ye may bring forth one who will make mention of Me amid My servants. This is My bidding unto you; hold fast to it as an assistance to yourselves". (19)

Dedicate one day to the Acknowledgement and Adoration of God, the Creator

The fourth Commandment given to Moses by God states: **"Remember the Sabbath day, and keep it holy... the seventh day is a Sabbath ... therefore the Lord blessed the Sabbath day and consecrated it".** (Exo. 20: 8,10-1) It became one of the most important commandments for the Jews, and from it evolved detailed rules defining what consisted work during the Sabbath and what labor could not be performed during this sacred day. One example suffices. Jewish leaders in Bethesda reprehended the crippled man, whom Jesus had cured on the Sabbath, for infringing the law because he was walking holding the bed on which he had previously lain! According to these leaders, **"It is the Sabbath and it is not lawful for you to carry your bed."** (Jn. 5:10) Rules became so burdensome and detailed that Jesus, himself, refutes the synagogue leaders who accused His disciples for working on the Sabbath because, as they walked through the grain fields, they were hungry and had plucked heads of grain to eat. Jesus silenced their arguments proclaiming that **"The Sabbath was made for man, and not man for the Sabbath"** (Mk. 2: 23-28).

If Jesus did not change the Sabbath as the day to adore God, He rescued the spirit and fundamental reason of its institution: a day to praise and publicly acknowledge God as the Creator of the Universe and the Creator of men with whom God had made a covenant to be their God and bless them as long as the people kept their end of the pact, which was to live according to His laws. If these Laws were obeyed, they would make their followers into 'sons of God'.

Zoroaster did not select a specific day in which to worship God. He took advantage of the fact that the Persians celebrated the longest night during the year, the winter solstice, around the 21st of December. The following day was observed as Sun Day, and Zoroaster dedicated it to Ahura Mazda, Supreme God, Wise Lord. Additionally, Zoroaster prohibited the animal sacrifices that previously were acceptable. (20)

The Catholic Church, using its alleged authority to interpret what God stipulated in the Ten Commandments, changed the of worship day from Saturday to Sunday. It is historically known that the change was instituted more for political reasons, in order to ingratiate the Church with the Roman Emperors who dedicated the Sun day (today Sunday) as the day of rest and worship to their god. Another reason for the change was that the first Christians, anxious to distance themselves from the Jews, and wanting not to be identified with them, selected Sunday as the Day of the Lord, since on this day Jesus was resurrected. Finally, in the year 364 AD at the Council of Laodicea, the Catholic Church proclaimed Sunday as the official obligatory day in which to worship God.

Mohammed decreed Friday would be the day to worship and praise God. This change was valid since God, through His Manifestation, Mohammed, was the one who modified the commandment to worship Him on the Sabbath, practiced by the Jews for more than a thousand years. The essential difference is that men did not make this decree as the one done by the Catholic Church. It was a modification done by a Manifestation.

Bahá'u'lláh modified the previous decree, no longer insisting on a particular day in which to meet and render praise unto God. Instead, He instituted a meeting of His followers every nineteen days within a nineteen month calendar year. This allows for the nineteenth day to fall on different days of the week. In these gatherings, there are no ministers, priests, rabbis or mullahs presiding. The Bahá'ís share prayers left to them by Bahá'u'lláh, discuss the progress of the community, and update each other on their faith-based activities during the past month, and discuss their daily activities as they experience their spiritual journey of Life.

Woman's equality to man

If there is something that has remained constant throughout the history of humanity until today, is the systematic abuse of woman by man. He has maintained an authoritative domination over her by the mere fact that he is a male and she is a female; that he is generally physically stronger than she is, and because, as long as he was a warrior, he was accustomed to imposing his will over the weaker ones, including the conquered women and ultimately his wife.

Similar to the ingrained tradition of slavery, was the inequality of men and women, as a by-product of many variables and circumstances. This inequality had been present since antiquity and thus the previous Manifestations did not make a commandment regarding the equality of man and women nor did they state that before God she had equal rights as men. Baha'ullah confronted this millenarian tradition of men's unequal treatment of women, because He foresaw that the male half of Humanity was mature enough to change his "macho" image (men don't cry; women do it all the time), which allowed them to see women as the weaker gender who needed to be 'guided', 'ordered', and 'maintained under control'.

Much had to change in customs and cultural beliefs before men began to consider that women had a relevant place in the life of the tribe, in professional life, in civic life, and the life of the country. Her being able to access these positions has been a long, long, slow, and painful process. It was, and continues to be today, a never-ending battle to achieve the gradual change in men's mentality, attitude of acceptance of the equality of women to men, and its corresponding expression in legislation.

Keeping this context as a frame of reference, Genesis – if taken literally - confirms this inequality from the moment of woman's creation, since she was made from one of Adam's rib, which in itself is already a manner of subordination to man, **"This is truly bone of my bones and flesh of my flesh."** (Gen. 2: 23) Thus, it is not surprising that woman, during the time of Moses and Israel's development as a nation, became a piece of her husband's property. She could not even bring any personal possession into the marriage, and could not inherit anything upon her husband's death. Instead, she and all his other worldly goods became property of the new husband (Num. 36: 6-9); she did not have the right to divorce whereas the man could divorce her by merely obtaining a judgment against her 'decency and purity'; additionally she could not defend herself of this accusation. (Deut. 24: 1)

A woman was basically excluded from all religious and civil activities because she was not allowed in the same area of the synagogue as men; she was not allowed to read or study the Torah; she was not permitted to enter the atrium of the Temple where men worshipped nor was she allowed to participate in gatherings when men defined civil behaviors. Moses's law evolved slightly when it came to giving woman protection when she was captured in war (Deut. 21:10...), when she was unjustly accused of having had sexual relations prior to marriage (Deut. 22: 13 ...), or in the case of rape (Deut. 22, 28...)

Yet, in the mist of such inequality, there are biblical stories in which a woman is the heroine, the one who maintains the faith in Yahweh, and the one who is superior to man. This is the case of Sarah, Hagar, Rebecca, Rachel and Leah, who played significant roles in the history of the people of Israel. In previous writings, Judith and Rachel are described as true heroines. But generally speaking, in the Old Testament, women's status before men did not improve significantly.

During the time in which Buddha appears in India, laws inherited from Hinduism did not substantially improve for status of women, especially during Manu, the most misogynous of

Brahmin legislators. In his Code of Laws he went as far as prohibiting "slave and women" from reading the sacred text of the Veda. He did not believe that woman, on her own merit, could reach Heaven; and since she was not allowed to perform any religious rituals, she remained a sinful being. In the words of Manu, **"Neither shame nor decorum, nor honesty, nor timidity is the cause of a woman's chastity, but the desire of a male alone."** (21) Therefore, it was necessary to keep women busy, so that they had no time for malfeasance or driving men to commit transgressions.

Nevertheless, in Buddha's original teachings women acquire a new level of respect that they did not have previously when He officially proclaimed that women, as well as men, could reach a state of illumination. In practice, this was translated in giving permission for some women to enter the Buddhist monastic orders as "bhikkhunis," a status subordinate to monks, as their servants.

Although Jesus, in his teachings, does not leave any explicit instructions regarding man's and woman's equality, He demonstrated through his words and actions the level of respect and acceptance women deserved. Judging by the number of miracles performed on women, Jesus clearly gave them a favored position: He cured a woman, who suffered from menstrual hemorrhaging for 12 years, (Mt. 9: 20-22) and the first person He resuscitated was the daughter of a Jewish official (Mt. 9: 22-26). It was to a Samaritan woman, ostracized by the Jews, to whom He revealed that He was the Messiah (Jn. 4: 7-26). He praised a widow in front of His disciples when He saw her placing her contribution, all she had, in the coffers of the Temple (Mk. 12: 41). He defended and protected a woman whom the Jewish leaders wanted to stone her to death because she was caught *in flagrante delicto* (Jn. 8: 1--11). He permanently shared His friendship and companionship with two sisters, Mary and Martha, who, although they were not publicly selected disciples, remained close to Him throughout the key moments of His life (Lk.10: 38-39). On His way to Calvary, He only addresses women weeping for Him (Lk. 23: 27-31).

There is only one male disciple next to the cross; the other two mourners are His mother and Mary Magdalene (Jn. 19, 25-27). Finally, it is to Mary Magdalene, not to his disciples, to whom He first appears resurrected (Mc 16: 9). These are clearly instances in which Jesus gave women the level of respect and standing they deserved within His Revelation.

Mohammed frames His vision of woman from the moment of her creation, insisting that she is equal to man's creation. This allows Him later to propose a further step in the evolution of man's thoughts and treatment of woman. When He elaborates on Creation in the Suras, He refers to women's status in the following terms:

> **"And that He it is Who causes death and gives life. And that He created pairs, the male and the female. From the small seed when it is adapted".** (22)

> **"Then he was a clot of blood, so He created (him) then made (him) perfect. Then He made of him two kinds, the male and the female".** (23)

> **"And the creating of the male and the female,"** (24)

In Mohammed's Revelation, improved conduct towards women is quite evident. The Koran states that a male as well as a female should inherit equally, something inconceivable at the time, by comparison to women in North America who did not acquire inheritance rights until the beginning of the 1900s. Nevertheless, the right of women to inherit is not total. It begins gradually because, according to the Hadiths, the portion inherited by the male should be twice that of the female. Clearly, this decree still favored man over the woman. (25) An additional progress in women's rights happened when Islam introduced the right of women to divorce, and advised them against remaining in an abusive relationship. The Koran recommends that both sides receive counseling prior to divorcing and allows their representatives to meet in order to resolve differences. Shariah, or Islamic law, sanctions divorce if reconciliation is not possible, but considers divorce undesirable if there are children involved. In the case of adultery, four witnesses are necessary, rather than the three required by Jewish Law; therefore, making it more difficult to condemn a woman.

Bahá'u'lláh's Revelation, like Mohammed, deals with the relationship from the very origin of woman's creation. It states emphatically that there is no difference between the creation of man and woman,

> **"O CHILDREN OF MEN!**
> **Know ye not why We created you all from the same dust? That no one should exalt himself over the other".** (26)

It is apparent that "dust" refers to the basic elements of the body (the same in both man and woman) which return to dust once we leave the temporary, physical world. And, in order to ensure that the basis of the origin is real, not metaphorical, 'Abdu'l-Bahá, when expounding this principle, he unequivocally affirmed:

> **"Know thou, O handmaid, that in the sight of Baha, women are accounted the same as men, and God hath created all humankind in His own image, and after His own likeness. That is, men and women alike are the revealers of His names and attributes, and from the spiritual viewpoint there is no difference between them".** (27)

Bahá'u'lláh proclaimed that "Women and men have been and will always be equal in the sight of God." (28) This affirmation implies that in God's creation of man and woman there was no justification that allowed half of the human race to acquire the right to abuse and repress the other half, by the only fact that half are men and the other half are women. There is no valid subordination of woman to man because in Bahá'u'lláh's words, **"God created women for men, and men for women"**. (29) To make sure there is no ambiguity in what He means, Bahá'u'lláh clearly states that this subordination and distinction is abolished in His new Revelation:

> **"In this day the divine grace has removed all distinctions. The servants and maidens of God are seen in the same station"**. (30)

Bahá'u'lláh's statements are unequivocal. They give a new definition of gender equality that previous Revelations had not provided. Women are not to be subordinated into a state of servitude, obliging them to suffering from systematic discrimination and dehumanizing oppression; they are not to be marginalized from civic processes that define how men and women live their daily lives in the nation.

There is a profound reason for this equality. Bahá'u'lláh's Revelation presents Humanity's next phase of spiritual progress; that is, the recognition and putting into practice of the Unity of mankind. Unity is not possible if half of Humanity is impeded from participating actively and fully in the development of the new civilization as designed by God for this day and age. Woman must be equal to man, having the same rights and privileges, as well as responsibilities, so that the unity of Humanity becomes a reality.

In his Testament, Bahá'u'lláh authorized his son, 'Abdu'l-Bahá, to interpret His writings, which He did do during His visits to North America and Europe. He was often posed questions regarding Bahá'u'lláh's new Revelation, which He answered in clear and concise terms. On the topic of the Unity of mankind He was emphatic in explaining that the creation of a new Humanity requires and demands equality between men and women. His words are amply explicit:

**"...man and woman are equally the recipients
of powers and endowments from God, the
Creator".** (31)

In this declaration, God does not make a spiritual distinction
between man and woman. God does not differentiate between
them because both were created in His "image and likeness".
In many of his writings, Bahá'u'lláh states that the 'likeness'
in His 'image' refers to the spiritual goal of humans, that of
developing his and hers God's given spiritual attributes, which
exclude sexual differences, being that God has no gender. In
the words of 'Abdu'l-Bahá:

> **"Know thou, O handmaid, that in the sight of
> Bahá, women are accounted the same as men,
> and God hath created all humankind in His
> own image, and after His own likeness".** (32)

This new Revelation grants man and woman equal status, from
their very origins of creation. It affirms that everyone has God's
attributes within themselves and that their purpose in life is to
reveal these attributes, equally and impartially. Again, in the
words of 'Abdu'l-Bahá:

> **"That is, men and women alike are the
> revealers of His names and attributes, and
> from the spiritual viewpoint there is no
> difference between them".** (33)

Obviously, this does not mean that someone can be superior
to others by virtue of his/her efforts to develop these attributes.
Yet, when 'Abdu'l-Bahá refers to this human ability, he is not
embarrassed to admit that in many occasions women surpass
men in this endeavor:

> **"Whosoever draweth nearer to God, that one
> is the most favoured, whether man or woman.
> How many a handmaid, ardent and devoted,
> hath, within the sheltering shade of Bahá,**

proved superior to the men, and surpassed the famous of the earth". (34)

The governing body of the Baha'i Faith, the Universal House of Justice, made a statement that amplifies and gives full context to this equality proclaimed by Bahá'u'lláh. It frames it in present day history, giving its much-needed projection:

> **"The emancipation of women, the achievement of full equality between the sexes, is one of the most important, though less acknowledged prerequisites of peace. The denial of such equality perpetrates an injustice against one half of the world's population and promotes in men harmful attitudes and habits that are carried from the family to the workplace, to political life, and ultimately to international relations. There are no grounds, moral, practical, or biological, upon which such denial can be justified. Only as women are welcomed into full partnership in all fields of human endeavour will the moral and psychological climate be created in which international peace can emerge."** (35)

The previous texts permit to see how the Revelation brought by each Manifestation is a spiritual advancement. Each Manifestation makes a judgment of the readiness of the group He addresses to learn a new lesson, which will bring about spiritual growth. Given that this is the reason that a Manifestation visits man, it is not surprising the He brings a new Revelation that is an advancement over the previous one. The new, renovated Revelation progresses beyond the past one, creating a dynamic process from which the concept of Progressive Revelation acquires its full meaning.

Based on what has been stated above, another conclusion arises: there is only one great Book of God's Revelation, and each religion that has appeared in history is a chapter of that book. So, one chapter in the book is titled "Hinduism", another, "Judaism", others, "Zoroastrianism", "Christianity", "Islam", and the most recent, the "Bahá'í" Faith. Only **one** continuous Revelation with many chapters, all complementary, all adapted to the reality and capacity of the people who received the particular Revelation at the moment in history in which the Manifestation appeared. A Progressive Revelation that has been there for Humanity from the time man appeared on Earth and will always be there, arriving in successive cycles, as 'Abdu'l-Bahá explained:

> **"Each of the Divine Manifestations has likewise a cycle, and during the cycle his laws and commandments prevail and are performed. When his cycle is completed by the appearance of a new Manifestation, a new cycle begins. In this way cycles begin, end, and are renewed, until a universal cycle is completed in the world, when important events and great occurrences will take place which entirely efface every trace and every record of the past; then a new universal cycle begins in the world, for this universe has no beginning".** (36)

The magnificence of the divine nature of the Manifestation has been made explicit. These celestial beings are way beyond any of our human categories. They reside in their own realm of Existence that is unattainable by any of us. Any relationship made with the Manifestation cannot be casual, nor can it be compared to the type of relationship one may have with a close friend or even a great leader. The status of the Manifestation, being the Spokesperson of God, demands that we have with Him a very special and unique contact. We shall examine in depth, in the next chapter, what kind of relationship is possible and desirable to have with the Manifestation.

Chapter 5
References

1) Bahá'u'lláh, *Gleanings from the Writings of Bấha'u'lláh,* XXXIV, p. 80
2) Ibid
3) Google. Thou shall not kill- Hinduismo. El *Hinduismo html.rincondelvago.com/el-hinduismo.html*
4) José Luis, Márquez, *Educadores de la Humanidad,* Y48.7, pg. 166
5) Buddist Ethic – Wikipedia Encyclopedia *es.wikipedia. org/wiki/Ética_budista*
6) Sura 17, 33
7) Bahá'u'lláh's "Kitáb-i-Aqdás", Paragraph 73
8) From a letter of the Universal House of Justice to the National Spiritual Assembly of Canada, May 26, 1969: Messages from the Universal House of Justice, 1968-1973.
9) El Bhagavad-Gita, Tal como es, traducción de Swami Prabhupada, The Bhaktivedanta Book Trust, 1978, pg. XXII
10) Korán 9, 29
11) Baha'u'llah, *The Summons of the Lord of Hosts,* p. 110
12) From a letter of the Universal House of Justice to the National Spiritual Assembly of Canada, May 26, 1969: Messages from the Universal House of Justice, 1968-1973.
13) BIC-*The Baha'i Question, Cultural Cleansing in Iran*, pg 27
14) Sura 60, 12
15) Sura 4, 161
16) Sura 4, 3
17) Sura 2, 229; 236
18) Bahá'u'lláh, The Kitáb-i-Aqdás, No, 63, p. 41
19) Bahá'u'lláh, The Kitáb-i-Aqdás, No, 63, p. 41
20) José Luis Márquez, *Educadores de la Humanidad,* pg.143

21) Google: The position of Women in Buddhism (*Laws of Manu,* trans. G. Buhler, *Sacred Books of the East,* Vol. XXV and IX, 10. (Oxford 1866) cited by L.S. Dewaraja, in *The Position of Women in Buddhism*; www. accesstoinsight. org /lib/ authors/dewaraja/wheel280. html

22) The Qur'an (E.H. Palmer tr), Sura 53, 44-46 - The Star

23) The Qur'an (E.H. Palmer tr), Sura 75 – 38-39 The Resurrection

24) The Qur'an (E.H. Palmer tr), Sura 92, 3 - The Night

25) Hadith - Qur'an 4: 11-12

26) Bahá'u'lláh, *The Arabic Hidden Words,* 68.

27) Compilations, The Compilation of Compilations vol II, p. 362, 2103. "Selections from the Writings of 'Abdu'l-Bahá" [rev. ed.], (Haifa: Bahá'í World Centre, 1982), sec. 38, pp. 79-80

28) Bahá'u'lláh The Compilation of Compilations vol II, p. 379, 2145

29) Bahá'u'lláh. Idem.

30) From a Tablet - translated from the Persian and Arabic) (Compilations, The Compilation of Compilations Vol. II, pg. 357

31) *"The Promulgation of Universal Peace"*: Talks Delivered by 'Abdu'l-Bahá during His Visit to the United States and Canada in 1912", pg. 300

32) Abdu'l-Bahá, *Selections from the Writings of Abdu'l-Bahá,* No.38. p. 79

33) Ibid, No. 38, pg. 80

34) Ibid. No. 38, pg. 79

35) The Universal House of Justice, Peace Statement, October 1985)

36) Abdu'l-Bahá, *Foundations of World Unity,* pg. 54

Chapter 6

Our Relationship to the Manifestation

As we discussed at the end of the previous chapter, the fact that a Manifestation is God's representative on Earth signifies that he is His Spokesperson. Therefore, we are not speaking of a mere mortal or spiritual leader; we are affirming that this person is as if God, Himself, were speaking to us. This fundamental fact differentiates the Manifestation from any human, placing Him within His own category of Being, inaccessible by any mortal, who - regardless of how much he tries - will never reach this level. Precisely because the Manifestation has reached this position, this loftiness in the Spirit, requires that we relate to the Manifestation in a way unlike any we have with another mortal. Let's examine the principal characteristics that this relationship implies.

Recognition

The first characteristic of the relationship one has with the Manifestation is that of fully-fledged recognition of who He is, who He represents, and where He comes from. Without acknowledging the holiness, the divinity of his origin, it is impossible to establish a true relationship. This recognition is the basis of the relationship and the reason why it is so special. Let's review once more the reasons that Bahá'u'lláh gives as to why we must acknowledge the elevated and independent station the Manifestation inhabits:

"Whoso recognizeth them hath recognized God. Whoso hearkeneth to their call, hath hearkened to the Voice of God, and whoso testifieth to the truth of their Revelation, hath testified to the truth of God Himself". (1)

The Divine origin of the Manifestation places Him within an elevated plane of existence inaccessible to any mortal. If we are facing God's representative at the moment of His appearance, the least we can do is recognize whom He is and whom He represents. No one is allowed in the King's court if that person denies that the one living inside is the King. No one is allowed into the Congressional Building if, from the outside, he proclaims that those inside are not the legitimate representatives of the people. No one establishes a real friendship with a stranger in the first encounter; one has to get to know that person intimately before considering him a true friend. A first step to establish a relationship with anyone is to acknowledge who he is, his origin, his title, his social role. In regards to the Manifestation the first step to get to know Him is to acknowledge that He is truly the Spokesperson and Representative of God on Earth.

Trust and Certainty

If recognition of the Manifestation's divine origin is the first step in establishing a relationship with Him, then the second step is trusting the reason for His coming.

To believe in a person, to have full confidence that we can count on him - such that we can share our innermost secrets - is born from the trust that the person inspires in us. The stronger the trust we have in the Manifestation, the stronger the possibility to confide in Him. When we gain this level of trust, we are ready to open our hearts to Him and confide our greatest fears, our miseries, and our hopes, our deepest doubts about life, death, the great beyond, and God.

Trust is the most precious offering that a Manifestation has for us. Out of it, we receive the firm conviction that He is not deceiving us, that He is not lying to us, that He is not hiding the truth from us. On the contrary, He presents himself as an open book willing to share with us what we yearn to hear about God. This trust turns into certainty that He is telling us the Truth about God.

A human being is most fragile when he or she is not certain that what he grasps via his five senses is real and not the product of his imagination. We hear gossip, or a lie about someone known, and, with minimal evidence, we may be swayed to think it is accurate, without confirming if what was said is true or not. We tend to give more weight to a rumor than to facts we know about the criticized individual; even facts indicating that such gossip is not true. This lack of certainty is perhaps the reason why we are never one hundred percent sure. What is affirmed by politicians, news broadcasters, magazine editorialists, or even by serious scholars and scientists is either true or it is merely the product of an over-stimulated or an overheated imaginations.

Thus, having the certainty that the Manifestation speaks God's Truth is a blessing; it gives us incredible peace and inner strength to defend that what He claims is Revealed Truth. But this certainty is based on our acknowledgement that He is, in fact, a true Manifestation of God, speaking in His name and not lying to us in what He is revealing about God. It is a certainty born from our trust that the Celestial Father will not fool us with false Revelations of Himself.

Adherence to Manifestation

If recognition of the divine origin of the Manifestation is the first step in establishing a relationship with him, a second step is trusting Him, then a third step follows almost immediately, and that is 'adherence to him'. The heart surrenders before the sublime station of the Manifestation. A bonding of the heart and mind with God's representative occurs and lasts until the appearance of the next Manifestation.

Something similar happens between lovers. The electric shock, the harmony of two hearts, and the bonding between them are simultaneous events. The loved one becomes the center around whom feelings of attraction and joy converge. Unconditional devotion results in overwhelming feelings when the loved one is near; her presence is an aroma that captures the senses, makes the heart flutter with happiness. It all leads to unrestricted, unlimited adherence to the person loved. The heart is surrendered and, with it, the whole being of the one who loves.

Natural bonding is spontaneous, arising as a volcano in the heart of a lover. One wishes to be with the loved one, without any type of prolonged separation. This continuous devotion must be sincere, spontaneous, acknowledged, as all love affairs are. Recognizing that one is in the presence of God's representative implies immediate surrender of one's heart, mind, and will.

Not bonding, not surrendering, not responding lovingly means rejection of, and distancing from the Manifestation. When this happens, the outcome is evident:

> **"Whoso turneth away from them, hath turned away from God, and whoso disbelieveth in them, hath disbelieved in God".** (2)

Being Thankful for His Life/Revelation

It is widely accepted that all the founders of today's religions have been accused of being false prophets (Moses, Jesus, Muhammad), have been persecuted (Moses, Zoroaster, Buddha, Jesus, Muhammad, The Báb, Bahá'u'lláh); struck (Zoroaster, Jesus, Muhammad, The Báb, Bahá'u'lláh); put into prison (Zoroaster, The Báb, Bahá'u'lláh); exiled (Buddha, Muhammad, Bahá'u'lláh); insulted (Moses, Jesus, Muhammad, The Báb, Bahá'u'lláh); accused without proof (Jesus, The Báb, Bahá'u'lláh); ridiculed, beaten and tortured (Moses, Jesus, Muhammad, The Báb, Bahá'u'lláh); executed (Jesus, The Báb) and assassinated (Zoroaster).

All this happened to them simply because they pronounced themselves to be messengers of God delivering the Revelation He was charged to give man. They offered their lives to God so that Revelation could be transmitted, knowing that they would suffer the humiliation, and the persecution because they accepted their Mission. They do this out of pure generosity and unconditional love for all who will be benefit from their sacrifice.

Remembering the sufferings endured by the Manifestations so that we could receive, through them, the Divine Light granted by God, we will be encouraged daily to be thankful for their unconditional love and gift of Revelation. Therefore, we should be forever grateful to the Manifestation for having graciously accepted the burden of the cross and carried it along the path of his mortal life, so that we would have abundant Eternal life in our fragile and fearful lives. Their lives are a permanent testimony to unselfish love that, in turn, elicits from us continuous praise and gratefulness.

Following the Manifestation

When one meets a Manifestation of God, the natural and logical thing to do is to follow Him wherever He takes you. This was blatantly obvious during Jesus' encounter with the first two disciples, when upon being asked where He dwelled, Jesus responded, "**Come and see." They came and saw where he was staying; and they stayed with him that day...**" (Jn. 1: 38-40) The irresistible attraction to the divine nature of Jesus produces a spontaneous and completely committed response from these new followers. A similar response occurs to anyone, with an open and sincere heart, when he comes in contact with the Manifestation; he immediately feels the desire to follow him.

Even Buddha, who did not set out to find followers, could not prevent enthused individuals from finding and joining him in practicing His teachings.

The Manifestation's sanctity of life, purity of action and way of life create such a strong force that those who behold His true nature cannot be held back. To follow Him wherever He goes becomes the reason for living. This was the case of Muhammad's first three disciples - his young cousin, Alí ibn Talib; his friend, Abu Bakr, and the young merchant, Uthman ibn Affan - who subsequently become pillars of early Islam and known warriors defending the Prophet.

The following is not only in the physical sense; it is more so in the heart, in thought and behavior. Once the follower acknowledges the wisdom and divine authority of the Manifestation, he becomes enamored with the ideas and precepts that the Voice of God is unveiling. His conviction progressively deepens as he understands more clearly the profundity of the Manifestation's teachings. Along with following, comes obedience to the new guidelines for living presented by the Manifestation. The teachings offered by the Manifestation have a fresh perspective. The new orientation is permeated with practical recommendations that apply to daily life and are attainable within the parameters of normal existence. The response of obedience to the new teachings translates into personal benefit since they show us the path to come closer to God, the ultimate reason of our creation. The more assured we are of this truth the easier it is to follow the teachings, not as arbitrary impositions, but as the surest means to achieving our ultimate end.

Proclaiming Him as a Manifestation

To follow a Manifestation implies proclaiming Who He is. It is not without reason that the media focuses daily on interviewing or reporting on public figures. These may include a known politician, an inventor, a Nobel Peace Prize winner, a courageous rescue hero; an activist arrested because of his convictions, a mother with meager resources who is raising two or three adopted children besides her own, or a preacher who inspires hope.

Before a reporter does an interview, he has done a thorough job of investigating. The reporter, asks where the interviewee was born, what did he study, what was his motivation for doing what he is interviewed about, who inspired him, what is the reason for supporting a specific cause? Thus, to properly showcase the interviewee and place him within the context of current events, reporters, at the time of the interview, become announcers that the lives of those presented merit observation, admiration, and, perhaps, following.

If we do this with our leaders and heroes, who are important, but are not transcendental beings as the Manifestations are, how can we remain silent and not proclaim to the entire world that we have had a recent visit from a Manifestation who has come to speak to us in the name of God and has given us a Revelation which can transform our individual and collective lives? How can we not want to announce His coming to all whom we meet in the path of life, if we are aware that sharing with them the Good News we are opening for them the possibility of transforming their own lives with the new Revelation?.

This is what His Holiness Jesus Christ's disciples did upon receiving the Holy Spirit. They left the house where they received Him filled with fervor and courage that is only possible to obtain after having had contact with the power of God present within the Manifestation. Let's remember the event:

> **"When the day of Pentecost had come, they were all together in one place. [2] And suddenly a sound came from heaven like the rush of a mighty wind, and it filled all the house where they were sitting. [3] And there appeared to them tongues as of fire, distributed and resting on each one of them. [4] And they were all filled with the Holy Spirit and began to**

speak in other tongues, as the Spirit gave them utterance". (Acts 2: 1-4)

Herein is the infusion of the Holy Spirit that Jesus promised. From it, the disciples received the strength and inspiration to proclaim who Jesus was, an audacious move that could have cost them their lives at the very moment of their testimony.

"Men of Israel, hear these words: Jesus of Nazareth, a man attested to you by God with mighty works and wonders and signs which God did through him in your midst, as you yourselves know— 23 this Jesus, delivered up according to the definite plan and foreknowledge of God, you crucified and killed by the hands of lawless men. 24 But God raised him up, having loosed the pangs of death, because it was not possible for him to be held by it". (Acts 2: 22-24)

Something comparable happened to Muhammad's followers who, convinced of the authenticity of the Prophet, did not hesitate to proclaim His Mission, putting their lives at risk. Similarly, when the followers of The Báb (precursor to the founder of the Bahá'í Faith) heard clearly His Proclamation, they embarked on a campaign to spread it across Persia. In doing so, they put themselves in jeopardy at the hands of the authorities of the Persian king and the religious leaders who wished to stifle them. The result was martyrdom of approximately 20,000 of The Báb's followers. This is the testimony of converted souls unafraid to proclaim the good news of the new Revelation.

The proclamation of the Manifestation's Revelation has normally been made by enthusiastic listeners, persuaded followers, dedicated preachers, generous missionaries, loving ambassadors, and unfortunately in some periods of history by religious wars and conquests carried out by military force. All these contributing factors made it possible for all the religions of the past to spread throughout the world. Today, they all claim a large number or followers who accept and proclaim the truthfulness of their corresponding Manifestation---Moses, Zoroaster, Buddha, Jesus, Mohammed, and Bahá'u'lláh.

Proclaiming the new message

What is unique about the relationship with a Manifestation is the invitation He extends to His followers to share His teachings, and Revelation with all wishing to hear "the good news". This was Jesus last directive, given to His followers when He ascended to meet His Father, **"And he said to them, "Go into all the world and preach the gospel to the whole creation."** (Mk. 16: 15)

This is the same calling that Bahá'u'lláh issues to His followers exhorting them to teach because it is God's will. He emphatically asserts, **"The Pen of the Most High hath decreed and imposed upon every one the obligation to teach this Cause..."** (3)

Nevertheless, this is not a recent request from God; Bahá'u'lláh clearly confirms that it has been His wish ever since He has spoken to humanity through His Manifestations.

> **"Indeed thou didst grasp the significance of rendering assistance unto God and didst arise to achieve this through the power of wisdom and utterance. Say: To assist Me is to teach My Cause. This is a theme with which whole Tablets are laden. This is the changeless commandment of God, eternal in the past, eternal in the future. Comprehend this, O ye men of insight".** (4)

Our relationship with the Manifestation acquires this new facet; we accept His invitation to teach the new Revelation because we are convinced that the "good news" that stem from God is the best news anyone can receive. As God does not keep the "Good News" to Himself, it is our task and duty to share those news with those who have not had the privilege or opportunity to listen to the new teachings firsthand.

The opportunity to teach the new Revelation demands that we follow certain logical conditions. The first is that no one can teach what one does not know. As such, one of the first steps is to immerse oneself in the new Revelation, learning it in depth so that one can transmit it with the deepest possible knowledge and profoundest understanding:

> **"God hath prescribed unto every one the duty of teaching His Cause. Whoever ariseth to discharge this duty, must needs, ere he proclaimeth His Message, adorn himself with the ornament of an upright and praiseworthy character, so that his words may attract the hearts of such as are receptive to his call".** (5)

In order to go out and share the new message, he who decides to teach is promised divine assistance. This was the case of Jesus' disciples who defied both Roman and Jewish authorities and spoke publicly about Him right after receiving the Holy Spirit on Pentecost day, **"And there appeared to them tongues as of fire, distributed and resting on each one of them. ⁴ And they were all filled with the Holy Spirit".** (Act.2: 3-4). In a similar manner, Bahá'u'lláh encourages those who have taken up His invitation to teach -- knowing that trust in God's assistance is what one needs to carry out the noble task of teaching. In His words:

> **"And when he determineth to leave his home, for the sake of the Cause of his Lord, let him put his whole trust in God, as the best provision for his journey, and array himself with the robe of virtue. Thus hath it been decreed by God, the Almighty, the All-Praised".** (6)

Clearly, besides the guarantee of divine assistance, those who responded to the calling must be aware of other personal requirements necessary to teach the Cause, such as readiness to be guided by the Holy Spirit, great determination, a mind completely focused on Him, and a generous heart:

> **"If they arise to teach My Cause, they must let the breath of Him Who is the Unconstrained, stir them and must spread it abroad on the earth with high resolve, with minds that are wholly centered in Him, and with hearts that are completely detached from and independent of all things, and with souls that are sanctified from the world and its vanities." (7)**

Service to Others, Service to the Cause of the Manifestation

If there are specific conditions under which teaching is most effective, it is no less important to understand clearly that **"opening the cities of the human heart"** is achieved through service. The great paradox of love lies in the measure with which it is bestowed. To give one's self, to share, to work for others is the key and the secret for approaching God. He has shared this secret with us through each Manifestation's teachings and exemplary life. Yet, this principle is so easily forgotten when the Manifestation returns to His heavenly abode. While we are enthralled with His presence, service is natural, spontaneous. But as soon as the Manifestation is gone and we go back to our daily struggle, amidst the challenge of survival, concern for others is difficult enough; doing service unto them borders on heroism, especially when we get a cold, indifferent, despondent response and rejection from those we wish to help.

During these moments, we must remember daily that service unto others is synonymous to serving the Cause of the Manifestation. The secret to remaining faithful and steadfast to the Manifestation happens when we follow His revealed teachings. They explain how worldly riches are fleeting in comparison to the rewards that will be bestowed upon those who faithfully respond to the invitation to teach. Nevertheless, to faithfully render service unto God requires absolute trust that one obtains the internal strength required to teach, when one trusts that the success of the teaching is placed on divine assistance rather than on one's own strength. Bahá'u'lláh expresses this spiritual reality succinctly:

> **"Wert thou to consider this world, and realize how fleeting are the things that pertain unto it, thou wouldst choose to tread no path except the path of service to the Cause of thy Lord. None would have the power to deter thee from celebrating His praise, though all men should arise to oppose thee".** (8)

Closeness to God is intimately tied to our relationship with others. Closeness to others is real when we serve them in their needs, both material as well as spiritual. One of the best ways to serve Bahá'u'lláh's Cause is by teaching His Revelation. Surprisingly, at the moment we chose to undertake this task, we are helping God execute His Plan for Humanity. Bahá'u'lláh explains it in these terms:

> **"Please God they may, one and all, be enabled to unlock, through the power of the Most Great Name, the gates of these cities. This is what is meant by aiding the one true God -- a theme to which the Pen of Him Who causeth the dawn to break hath referred in all His Books and Tablets."** (9)

But we know that working for this or any other cause is not without effort. This is evident in any enterprise that is undertaken, regardless of its purpose and meaning. All human endeavors require exertion. We can recall Jesus' words when He extended the invitation to those who had come to listen to him, **"Whoever does not bear his own cross and come after me, cannot be my disciple".** (Lk. 14, 27) Following the Manifestation requires treading on a narrow path while carrying the weight of responsibility that the challenge entails. Nevertheless, victory is assured to the extent that the objective remains clear. Bahá'u'lláh explains in these terms:

> **"Considering this most mighty enterprise, it beseemeth them that love Him to gird up the loins of their endeavor, and to fix their thoughts on whatever will ensure the victory of the cause of God..."** (10)

The effort inherent in this chore is not different to that required by any other human task. The big difference is the genuine conviction, the trust placed on Him who can speak for us. When teaching is done this way, those who listen will be positively influenced. Again, in Bahá'u'lláh's words:

> **"It behoveth them to choose as the best provision for their journey reliance upon God, and to clothe themselves with the love of their Lord, the Most Exalted, the All-Glorious. If they do so, <u>their words shall influence</u> their hearers".** (11) – (underline by author)

All that we have analyzed until now --- that God has spoken, non-stop, to Humanity through His Manifestations, in human terms which we can understand, thus fulfilling God's permanent desire to communicate with us. He does so because He has a Master Plan for Humanity: to send us saintly luminaries to light up the paths that we, as individuals and as members of humanity, should follow. We are to follow them because they show us the ultimate goal of our existence: to arrive at God's presence where our thirst for the Infinite and Immortality will be completely fulfilled. In the next chapter, we will attempt to summarize the grand scheme of God's Plan.

Chapter 6
References

1) Bahá'u'lláh, *Gleanings from the Writings of Baha'u'llah*, XXI, pg. 49
2) Baha'u'llah, *Gleanings from the Writings of Baha'u'llah*, XXI, p. 49
3) Bahá'u'lláh, *Gleanings from the Writings of Baha'u'llah*, CXLIV, pg. 313
4) Baha'u'llah, *Gleanings from the Writings of Baha'u'llah*, p. 196
5) Bahá'u'lláh, *Gleanings from the Writings of Baha'u'llah*, CLVIII, p. 335
6) Bahá'u'lláh, *Gleanings from the Writings of Baha'u'llah*, CLVII, pg. 333
7) Bahá'u'lláh, *Gleanings from the Writings of Baha'u'llah*, C, pg. 200
8) Bahá'u'lláh, *Gleanings from the Writings of Baha'u'llah*, CXLIV, pg. 313
9) Bahá'u'lláh, *Gleanings from the Writings of Baha'u'llah*, CXV, pg. 241
10) Bahá'u'lláh *Gleanings from the Writings of Baha'u'llah*, CXV, pg.242
11) Bahá'u'lláh, *Gleanings from the Writings of Baha'u'llah*, C, pg.200

Chapter 7

God's Plan

A comparison may prove useful before we tackle the grand scheme of God's Master Plan for Humanity. The role that a father plays with his son as he is growing up is similar to the relationship God has with us. As always, all analogies suffer limitations, and, therefore, are not perfect. Nevertheless, this one provides an excellent basis from which we can explore God's Plan for Humanity.

Role of a father

Let's take the case of an honorable, hard working man, thoughtful, totally dedicated to his work and family. By the time he reaches maturity, he has acquired sound life experience: he has managed to know what works, what doesn't, what brings about unhappiness, what aids personal growth, what provides peace and joy. Around age thirty, the man marries an excellent woman who, besides having marvelous personal qualities, has also gained wisdom about life from individual experiences as well as those shared with friends. Both hope to have children to whom they can teach these experiences in a way that each child will develop his/her own potential, growing up not only independent and self-sufficient but contributing greatly to humanity.

In fact, Life gives them the gift of a son and a daughter. The parents bestow on them extraordinary love and affection, focusing on each moment of their growth cycle to offer the support, understanding, and guidance, so they can grow up healthy developing their abilities, skills and personalities.

As they grow, their children go through the usual stages of development: from infancy to childhood, to adolescence, and then youth. During each stage, these parents maintain intense, sincere, and open communication with their children. This communication helps the parents to guide their children's steps so that they learn what is good and what is evil, what is ugly and what is beautiful, what is just and what is unjust, what is painful and what is enjoyable, how to behave with friends, how to forgive when one is offended, how to abstain from hurting someone, how to serve without expecting something in return.

All children's learning moments are played out against a backdrop of experience. Both parents are conscious that certain choices, made early on, may have disastrous consequences, and to continue making such choices may crush the best dreams one may have as a youth. Alcohol is one such experience. Both parents have experienced the tragedy of a friend who at some point of his/ her life started drinking socially without ever intending to drink on a continuous basis. But the environment in which the friend lives is conducive to meeting others, who are not preoccupied with the serious side of life, and who often and regularly resort to alcohol in order to try to feel "cool", free of worry, removed from the stress of daily living. To the extent that, in order not to deal with these pressures, alcohol consumption increases and becomes the escape door, rather than facing such stress rationally, with a cool head and critical analysis. Obviously, the ability for reflective thinking becomes impaired in youngsters under the influence of alcohol.

Therefore, both parents explain in detail, he to the son, she to the daughter, how women and men begin drinking alcohol, the immediate effects it has on their mind and mental capacity, how loss of self-control may lead to violent reactions or unchecked rampant emotions can result having sex with someone they barely know. The parents discuss with them the circumstances that make up their everyday life such as their search for status, and group acceptance; the ever- present peer pressure and dares made by companions; the celebration of camaraderie or small successes through drinking; the feeling that drinking is a requisite to making friends. The parents point out how all of these instances create an environment within which group dynamics trap and engulf them, pushing them to behave in ways they know are not acceptable and have negative consequences.

These parents understand well the consequences of drinking. They have seen close friends destroyed by alcohol, taking away their potential of becoming the giants that Life had invited them to be. Therefore they spare no opportunity to inform, talk, exchange ideas, and enlighten their children as to the consequences they will fall prey to if they choose to drink. To put the decision in balance, these parents present their children the greater benefits they will obtain by abstaining from drinking making an effort to put into context how the apparent joy and frivolity exhibited by their friends or by themselves, under the influence of alcohol, is no more than a fleeting moment of artificial happiness that evaporates as soon as they are sober.

Are the efforts displayed by these concerned parents prohibitions, restraining orders, arbitrary restrictions on their children's liberties, subjugation to the will of the parents, or are they sure guide lines needed to avoid life's pitfalls?

At no time do these parents seek to restrain their children, to dominate them, or control their lives. Clearly what these parents want for the children is that in an informed manner and using their freedom, they understand and accept the harmful consequences that alcohol brings to their lives; and, consequently, to opt not to consume it. Obeying for the sake of obeying or because parents have the upper hand is irrational obedience. The reason for obeying should not be the result of parents prohibiting children from doing something, but rather, it should be the response of children who, reflecting upon the potential destructive effects of any addiction, realize its crushing consequences and based on the potential negative results decide freely not to consume alcohol, drugs or any other substance offered as a passing recreation.

The Role of God

We are now ready to make the analogy between God and ourselves, His utmost creation.

First of all, God, as Creator, is directly our Father, much as we, in an analogous way, give birth to our own children and then consciously or unconsciously, mold them "in our image and likeness". God, having created us moved by His Love and wanting to share His Divinity with us (understating it as God's attributes imbedded in our soul) has developed a very special relationship with us. This relationship becomes apparent in the temporal world as a connection, a movement, a heartfelt and intimate feeling of closeness to Him. It is there where we feel God's presence, and that is why we express metaphorically that God "dwells in the heart of man".

David (foreshadow of Jesus according to Old Testament scholars) expressed wonderfully clear how nothing escapes God's intimate knowledge of the human's heart when he exclaimed in his Psalm, **"Would not God search this out? For He knows the secrets of the heart."** (Ps. 44:21)

Jesus used the same heart metaphor to point out that it is in the heart where man decides whether or not to accept the Messenger sent by God. He did so when He defied the Pharisees in the temple by curing a man's lame hand on the Sabbath and, thus, exposing the hardness of their hearts,

> "And when He had looked around at them with anger, being grieved by the hardness of their hearts, He said to the man, "Stretch out your hand". And he stretched it out, and his

hand was restored as whole as the other".
(Mk, 3: 5-6)

Muhammad also points out to the special role man's heart plays in his relationship with Allah, because it is there that faith first enters: **"The dwellers of the desert say: We believe. Say: You do not believe but say, We submit; and faith has not yet entered into your hearts"**, (1). and, additionally, Allah sees the intimacy of each one's heart, **"Allah knows what is in your hearts; and Allah is Knowing, Forbearing"**. (2)

Bahá'u'lláh asserts that man's heart belongs exclusively to God, and it is man's heart's capacity to love that He wants:

> **"Give a hearing ear, O people, to that which I, in truth, say unto you. The one true God, exalted be His glory, hath ever regarded, and will continue to regard, the hearts of men as His own, His exclusive possession"**. (3)

It is because of his closeness, his special attention and exclusive love for man that Bahá'u'lláh states, **"The one true God, exalted be His glory, hath ever regarded, and will continue to regard, the hearts of men as His own, His exclusive possession"**. (4) It is this high degree of intimacy that He wishes to have with all of us, His children, made in his "own image and likeness". This is the prerogative that any creator has with his work, similar to the one a parent has with his own children. Each parent is responsible for guiding his child to fulfill the purpose of his creation, that of improving the world he presently inhabits by serving others, inspiring them to express the best of themselves.

God, being Who He is, Self-sufficient, Omniscient, Creator, has eternal experience, and thus always knows what is best for us, what is best for all of creation. As the author of Creation, God knows, not only the purpose for which we are created, but what is most convenient for each one of us. Because we are created in His "image and likeness", we carry the stamp of divinity within our being, within our soul. Therefore, God, better than anyone, knows the ultimate reason for which He created us; that is, to return to Him in order for us to enjoy eternally in His presence, in a state of indescribable joy, abundance, and complete self-realization. This is His master Plan for us. He knows which path best suits us to make that Journey back to Him while we are in this temporary world, as He knows what path is best for us once we cross over past this time-space constraint and truly begin our journey into immortality.

Precisely because God knows the reason why He created us, He has constantly, throughout history, let us know what our goal is as beings created in His "own image and likeness". He does so by showing us the path, the route, and the way most conducive to reaching such an end. These signals are His rules for living, the behaviors we should carry out in harmony with nature and others, the ethical and moral prescriptions by which we can awaken, enliven and fortify our spiritual powers, the ones that propel us toward the goal for which we were created, but that we must laboriously discover. No one can travel across a strange country without a map, without asking questions, seeing signs, and receiving indications and directions where to go. The map we need is the content of the Revelation that the Manifestation brings us. It also gives us the instructions on how to live our lives in the right direction. The content of the Revelation allows us to develop in a way that our internal growth can bring about the abundance that Jesus foretells, "**I have come that they may have life and that they may have it more abundantly**". (Jn. 10:10)

God's Plan

God's Plan consists in sending humanity, from time to time, a Manifestation who, being His Spokesperson, delivers to the people He addresses a complete Revelation. The content of the Revelation becomes the best guide and map to follow the path that will allow its recipients to attain the purpose for which they were created.

Each specific Revelation is a component of the Master Plan that has invited all human beings, from the beginning of time, those inhabiting Earth today, and those of future centuries, to reach the intended goal of their existence. All are invited to return to their place of origin, God Himself. This goal has been known throughout history as Paradise: a state of unending happiness and plentitude, a state of unending peace, a feeling of accomplishment, and an awareness that allows us to understand the mysteries or the universe. All these images have helped us to articulate, to affirm something about the indescribable state of bountifulness, of unlimited joy that we will one day experience in His presence.

We will reach this goal if we follow the path He has traced for us, if we use the Guide He has sent us in order not to get lost, if we implement the advice that God the Father has given us, His children, so that we can reach our full potential. But, as a parent who loves us without restriction, He allows us to freely decide whether or not to accept the advice and guidance He has given us through His Manifestation. Our freedom of choice will permit us to seek out the reasons that help us understand why God has proposed that we carry out the behaviors that will benefit our spiritual development the most. This liberty of choice gives us also the alternative to flatly reject His guidance on the grounds that it is a "limitation to our liberty", or an "obedience forced on us by His authority", or a "whim of God."

Within this great Plan, each people have a historical role to play in the evolution of Humanity. Every group has a particular role to fulfill because each contributes something specific to the spiritual, moral, and ethical inheritance of Humanity. This unique feature is wrapped up within the specific Revelation that any particular group receives and contributes to the universal 'collective understanding" of God's Essence, His Attributes, His presence in our lives, His role as Creator, His specific plan for each person.

In order to fulfill His Plan, God has resorted to something very human, making a pact. It is a commitment mechanism as old as man himself. It has been and remains the common mode of reaching an agreement with someone - even the enemy. It is the means by which certain rules are followed and conditions are articulated for a specific purpose, a goal both parties agree on. In time of war between two countries, the treaty can be a document that establishes the behavior of the winner over the loser, what rights are still maintained by the defeated, what are the privileges of the victor.

In peacetime, negotiations are established to pool economic, material and human resources for the purpose of achieving a goal such as the construction of a tunnel through a mountain bordering two nations to avoid building a longer, winding road at increased expense and time. There can also be commercial agreements to decrease costs, share routes, or transport vehicles in order to prevent their wear and tear. Technical partnerships are established to invent a new pharmaceutical product for worldwide distribution or to develop a polymer compound in a product whose success is virtually guaranteed.

These few examples illustrate how we continually make agreements with the clear goal of obtaining something that is mutually beneficial to the parties engaged. God, in accordance with our ways of managing our relationships, similarly resorts to a pact, in order to establish a 'modus operandi' with us. As far as He is concerned, we have the firm and fixed guarantee that He will always keep His promise to never leave us without a Guide or support. God supports us at each instance of our return journey to the House of the Father. He will always be there for us, when we ask for enlightenment, when we ask for strength to continue walking, but above all, always illuminating our route with the clear signals and indications that we need to stay on the course that will lead us to our ultimate goal.

We implement those signals and guidelines when we follow the pact that God makes with us. We agree to openly and fearlessly proclaim that we follow those guidelines and instructions because He is our Father and wishes the best for us. It is for this reason that He has given us a clear indication of what is

His Plan, which will guide us in our return Journey to the Father. We accept the invitation, study the instructions, find reasons why they are beneficial and put them into practice. If we keep our part of the pact we are guaranteed we will reach the goal of arrival in Paradise.

God's Plan, throughout each Manifestation, is to make a pact with the people He reveals Himself to being faithful to them always. In turn, those accepting to live according to the divine, ethical, moral and social precepts given to them by the Manifestation are guarantee to be receiving the surest, most fitting path to fulfill the purpose for which each one is created.

The Manifestation's divine force stimulates development

God's Plan has a material and practical result for the people who enter into an agreement with God. We have stated that the Manifestation, because He is who He is, is the representative of God on Earth, and has within Himself the creative power of the Divine Word, which is ultimately the means by which God creates the universe and man. His Creative Word has the strength and power to initiate the creative processes of those He addresses. Shoghi Effendi, Bahá'u'lláh's great grandson, explained it this way:

> **"The Call of God, when raised, breathed a new life into the body of mankind, and infused a new spirit into the whole creation. (4)**

This power is apparent in the blossoming of modern man's intellectual and creative capacities in a way that seems as if entire nations are awaken to a higher evolutionary phase. In a mysterious and seemingly magical way, new ideas and incredible inventions arise everywhere that lighten our daily loads and elevate the quality of our lives to heights never reached before.

This creative drive has produced multiple new inventions as never seen in past history, such as: gas stoves, electric water heaters, microwave ovens, appliances to make juice from any fresh fruit or vegetable; all type of machines to clean the house---from the simple broom of plastic fibers to the most sophisticated vacuum cleaners; clothes washers and industrial irons. We can control lights automatically, detect smoke to prevent fires; we have burglar alarms, schedule automatic garden sprinklers and use a remote control to open a garage door. There are many new means of transportation on the surface of the earth, on water, in the air, devouring kilometers, some traveling faster than the speed of sound.

Modern man has made devises that measure temperature and density of objects, that take photographs of clouds and track the development of storms and hurricanes; he has made tools to create color maps that reveal mineral deposits hidden below the surface of the earth; machines than can perforate, bore through, disembowel, and violate Earth in search of precious stones and minerals such as gold and silver and fossil fuels such as coal and petroleum.

We have made new tools that penetrate the skin and show what lies inside human organs; used radioactive elements to treat tumors and abnormal growths. Modern man has made are apparatus that analyze bodily fluids and others that examine internal organs to detect the presence of microorganisms causing chronic or deadly illnesses. These machines perform the seemingly impossible a few years ago.

In the ultra small world revealed by powerful microscopes, scientists have discovered structures resembling a haunted and majestic tropical jungle showing a multitude of designs, multicolored patterns, intricate form combinations, and luxurious groupings. Present day humans have jumped from the microscopic to macroscopic world, investigated the unreachable depths of the universe using the Hubble, the most powerful space telescope (1966), and have photographed the birth of a star and a mantle of deep space sprinkled with hundreds of uncharted galaxies. We have sent space probes and remote controlled robots such as the one sent to Mars in

July of 1997[3] to analyze the composition of rocks that suggests that at some remote time Mars had water and, therefore, the possibility of some form of life.

Astronauts, suspended over Earth and tied to the Discovery spaceship by a platinum umbilical cord, have done repairs on damaged satellites, have carried out maintenance jobs on the international space station, or substituted a part on the Hubble space telescope. They have done these tasks giving the impression they are minor endeavors when such tasks are major spacewalks achievements, impossible to have dreamed on doing at the beginning of the space program.

There is no area of expertise in which modern humans have not used their inquisitive nature and discovered, designed, manufactured, and made to work inventions that have permitted him to dominate, bend and harness the gigantic forces of nature to satisfy basic necessities and reach new levels of comfort. Torrents of water accelerate turbines to create electricity, entire forests of gigantic hundred-year-old trees are chopped, cut, and reduced to wood planks to build homes, furniture, toys, ornaments, and utensils. Fossil fuels have been extracted from the depths of the Earth to be converted into fuel for industry. Cement foundations have been laid to sustain impressive skyscrapers and monumental bridges. Rivers and canals are excavated to provide passageways for ships of deep draft that carry thousands upon thousands of consumer goods (some necessary, some superfluous) from port to port.

One feels a wave of modern inspiration that results in incredible designs and paintings by artists who beautify buildings with majestic murals and give life to epic events in history. Modern statues capture the sublime moment of human endeavors, during war or peacetime, trapping within them the historical significance of the particular event, or simply capturing the magic of a daily scene such as children playing in a park.

---

[3]   El Tiempo, Julio 9, 1997, 1

New philosophical currents arise in Europe, and in the Americas exploring the mysteries of being human, our potential, and our relationships amongst each other in new levels of co-existence. New religious treatises are now written about topics never postulated previously. Fabulous novels are written, which capture the spirit of an entire era or simply show the complexity of our psyche. New education models are implemented, traditions that were untouched for millennia are questioned, and alternatives to present government structures are proposed.

These advances are happening at the material as well as the spiritual level promoting the maturity of humanity, enabling it to achieve higher degrees of unity even though the signs are yet weak but are present to those that can discern the presence of the Spirit changing the world on an almost daily basis.

Most of present day innovations have come about because there has been a re-birth of human creative power, which can be traced as happening mostly during the 19th- 20th Century and going on stronger in the beginnings of the 21st Century. The wave of innovations started with the appearance of Baha'u'llah and his prediction that such creative power was going to be infused in the world. The force of the Creative Word of the Manifestation goes beyond those who hear directly His new Revelation. Those who have not heard it experience its effects and even contribute unknowingly to the creation of a powerful civilization, which did not exist previously.

The growth and flourishing of the new civilization, the development of extraordinary capabilities of its members occur despite the failure of humans to be faithful to the new Revelations. God is always faithful; man, on the other hand, is always breaking his promises. God has boundless capacity to forgive and sublime patience to wait until we mature and His Plan takes effect, regardless of how many times He must extend His hand to help us get back on our feet when we fall.

We are now ready to appreciate the arrival of Bahá'u'lláh, God's most recent Manifestation in the history of Humanity. Although we have already quoted him or alluded to the fact that He is a Manifestation based on the terms we defined previously, it is now appropriate to introduce Him formally in our next chapter.

Chapter 7
References

1) Sura 49, 14.
2) Sura 33, 51:
3) Bahá'u'lláh, *Gleanings from the Writings of Bahá'u'lláh*, CII. p. 206
4) Shoghi Effendi, *The World Order of Baha'u'llah*, p. 169

Chapter 8

The most recent Manifestation

We have explained how God has never left Humanity without a Teacher, without a Manifestation to guide it through its next phase of its spiritual growth. If so, should we ask ourselves, was Mohammed the last known Prophet who started a new religion? Has no other Manifestation appeared in recent history?

Arrival of the New Manifestation

As the reader can now construe, a new Manifestation has appeared in man's recent history. His name, as we mentioned previously, is Bahá'u'lláh, meaning "the Glory of God" in Arabic. He was born in Tehran, Persia, in 1817 and was given the name of Husayn-'Ali. As one of the chief counselors of the King of Persia, His father was highly regarded and the family enjoyed a comfortable economic status.

From an early age, Bahá'u'lláh,

> **"was extremely kind and generous. He had an extraordinary power of attraction, which was felt by all. People always crowded around Him. Ministers and people of the Court would surround Him, and the children also were devoted to Him. When He was only thirteen**

or fourteen years old He became renowned for His learning",

despite having had minimal formal education. (1)

Around the same time, many Christians, in various parts of the world, were anxiously awaiting the return of Jesus Christ, as well as Islam, which was expecting the arrival of the "Twelfth Imam". Christians and Muslims affirmed that their scriptures announced the advent of a new spiritual era to be ushered in by a new Manifestation.

Nineteen years before Bahá'u'lláh proclaimed himself a Manifestation, a 25-year old young man, known by His followers as The Báb, declared on May 23, 1844 that He was the promised Qá'im of Islam. Qá'im means "He who has arisen" and was awaited by Muslims for 1,260 years. The Báb means "the Door" or "the Gate" in Arabic. The Báb explained that He was the Gate by which God's long awaited Revelation would come forth into the world. The central theme of his most well-known book, *The Bayan*, revolves around the appearance of a new Messenger of God, more eminent than The Báb himself, who's Mission would be to bring about the peace and justice proclaimed by Islam, Judaism, Christianity and all other major religions.

To learn more about the Bahá'í Faith, its perspective on previous religions, its understanding of the present world situation and its vision of the future, visit the web page: http://www.bahai.org

The Báb referred to the arrival of this Divine Master as "**Him Whom God shall make manifest**" and affirmed, "**that no words of Mine can adequately describe Him, nor can any reference to Him in My Book, *The Bayan*, do justice to His Cause**". (2)

The Báb claimed that, "**The purpose underlying this Revelation, as well as those that preceded it, has, in like manner, been to announce the advent of the Faith of Him Whom God will make manifest**". (3) Likewise, He explained that the basis of all human advancement must be found in the teachings of God's Universal Manifestation, and that "**the sum total of the religion of God is but to help Him,**" (4) According to The Báb, humanity had reached the next stage of development and He was no more than the voice "**... and He, verily, hath cried out in the wilderness of the Bayan**" announcing to Humanity its progress towards collective maturity. (5)

Despite the fact that The Báb repeatedly declared himself Bahá'u'lláh's Herald, He was equally a true Spokesperson of God. In a letter to Mullah Husayn, the first to recognize Him as Islam's anticipated One, The Báb confirms that He is a Manifestation of God, speaking in His name:

> "**Say: All matters must be referred to the Book of God; I am indeed the First to believe in God and in His signs; I am the One Who divulgeth and proclaimeth the Truth and I have been invested with every excellent title of God, the Mighty, the Incomparable. Verily I have attained the Day of the First Manifestation and by the bidding of the Lord and as a token of His grace, I shall attain the Day of the Latter Manifestation**". (6)

It is for this reason that His appearance within the context of previous Manifestations is of particular importance. Besides being the herald of Bahá'u'lláh, as an authentic Manifestation,

He had his own Mission. The appearance of The Báb "... at once signalized the termination of the "Prophetic Cycle" and the inception of the 'Cycle of Fulfillment', "of which Bahá'u'lláh was to be its central figure. (7)

In a certain sense the role of The Báb is comparable to that played by John the Baptist as broadcaster of the imminent coming of the Messiah expected in Judaism, being that John the Baptist, much like The Báb, recognizes the superior status of the one whose arrival he announces. John had no problem acknowledging this when he said to his followers:

"I indeed baptize you with water; but One mightier than I is coming, whose sandal strap I am not worthy to loose. He will baptize you with the Holy Spirit and fire". (Lk.3: 16-17)

Similarly, The Báb, although being a true Manifestation, was not only a broadcaster like John, but the Herald of Bahá'u'lláh. His main mission was to pave the way for the arrival of Bahá'u'lláh, as John the Baptist did for Jesus. Consequently, the foundation of the Bahá'i Faith is regarded by Bahá'is as simultaneous to the Bábí Faith, whose reason for being would culminate in 1863 when Bahá'u'lláh announced that He was the personage promised by The Báb "**... chosen to be the Herald of His Name and the Harbinger of His Great Revelation..**". (8)

When The Báb appeared, He did so with the same magnetism as the other previous Manifestations. The force of His words and the revolutionary message calling for spiritual renewal, the promotion of education, and the sciences captured the attention of whoever listened to Him. The Báb's announcement was that of an entirely new religion that allowed the listeners to make a break with Islam and prepare themselves for the arrival of the one proclaimed by Him. Some of the followers, such as Mullá Husayn who listened to Him in person, were able to respond immediately to His invitation to join Him as a disciple. A follower who went to visit Him while He was confined in the Máh-Kú prison, located in Ádharbáyján, a province in the northwest of Iran, superbly described the enchanted effect of The Báb's voice:

"The melody of His chanting, the rhythmic flow of the verses which streamed from His lips caught our ears and penetrated into our very souls. Mountain and valley re-echoed the majesty of His voice. Our hearts vibrated in their depths to the appeal of His utterance." (9)

This is the effect of God's transforming Word, present in His Manifestation, when received by those who listen to Him.

The overwhelming potency of The Báb's words spread like wildfire throughout Persia with such force and power of attraction that the clergy of the time viewed this charismatic young man as a threat to their position and power. If He was, in truth, the eagerly awaited Qá'im, they would have to acknowledge Him as such and become His followers, at the expense of giving up their privileged positions they held as spiritual and political leaders of Islam. This staunch defense of their privileges becomes evident in contrast to Bahá'u'lláh's reaction upon receiving a letter from The Báb; without doubting for a moment, He recognized The Báb as a true Manifestation from God. Despite not ever meeting The Báb personally, Bahá'u'lláh became one of His best well-known followers.

The Báb's extraordinary power of attraction convinced dozens, then hundreds, then thousands of enthusiastic followers. Facing the alarming growth of new converts, known as Bábis, the rulers and representatives of the clergy made the decision to curtail the expanding new Faith. They sent out, countrywide, an order to shut down the new Faith. As a result, The Báb was imprisoned. Nevertheless, the movement continued to grow, thanks to the courageous and wholeheartedly dedication of His first eighteen disciples, known as the *"Letters of the Living"*, each one of them had independently accepted The Báb as the new Manifestation without knowing that the others had done the same. Once all 18 acknowledged Him, The Báb sent them throughout Persia proclaiming the new Faith, announcing that He was the expected Qá'im. They did so with such conviction and enthusiasm that soon a deep religious revolution was taking place in all of Persia.

It did not take long for the clergy and ruling class to unleash a full scale persecution upon the Bábís; thousands were martyred during the course of a horrific chain of killings. The extraordinary valor shown by the Bábís while being assaulted by the Shah's military forces did not escape notice from numerous Western observers. European intellectuals such as Ernest Renán, León Tolstoy, Sarah Bernhardt, and the Count of Gobineau. They were profoundly affected by the savage persecution developing in a country considered to be immersed in deep religious obscurantism.

The religious leaders and government officials who opposed The Báb accused him not only of being a heretic but also as a dangerous rebel. The authorities decided to end his life, and on July 9, 1850, the sentence was carried out. In one of the courtyards of the military headquarters in Tabriz, nearly ten thousand people crowded the town's main plaza and the top of the roofs of homes and buildings surrounding it. The Báb and Anis Zunuzi, a 19-year old follower who had volunteered to die with The Báb, were tied to ropes knotted to a ring fastened to a wall of the plaza.

Sam Khan, a Christian officer in charge of the regiment that was to execute The Báb, recognized him as a saintly man, and, therefore, did not want to follow this order and communicated his dilemma to The Báb. The Báb assured him that if he would place his trust in God, he would be free of his responsibility. Trusting The Báb, he ordered a regiment of 750 Armenian soldiers, divided into 3 lines of 250 men, to fire upon the prisoners. The smoke produced by the muskets' gunpowder was so intense that the entire courtyard was covered by a dark cloud.

After the cloud of smoke dissipated, the crowd was stunned to see that Anis was completely unharmed, and that The Báb had disappeared. A frantic search of His whereabouts began. He was finally found in His cell finishing dictating to his secretary the letter that was interrupted by the guard who dragged Him to the execution plaza. It was necessary to bring in a second regiment of 750 soldiers, comprised of only Moslems, because Sam Khan refused to have his regiment fire again on the prisoners since he had already carried out the execution orders. The new brigade brought in fired their muskets, and this time both bodies were torn to shreds, except for their faces.

After The Báb's execution, Bahá'u'lláh's extraordinary personality, intelligence, leadership, deep spirituality, lofty virtues of compassion, detachment, and generosity attracted The Báb's followers who turned to Him as the natural leader of the expanding group. This angered government officials, who in turn, redoubled their efforts to extinguish the flame of the new religion as soon as possible.

In 1852 they arrested Bahá'u'lláh and incarcerated him in a dungeon prison made out of deep storage wells for Teheran's public baths. It was known as the "Black Pit" because it was so dark that no light reached the prisoners, because it was three stories underground. The prisoners were shackled to the walls and to each other without access to any hygienic facilities forcing them to share the dark enclosure with vermin and their own body wastes.

It was in this prison that Bahá'u'lláh received God's Revelation from the Celestial Maiden, symbolic of the "Greatest Spirit", who announced to Him that He was the Promised One of all religions. Bahá'u'lláh did not mention this Revelation to any of his prison mates or anyone else, until it was the right moment, ten years later in Baghdad before He was exiled again to Constantinople.

After four months in the Black Pit, the Persian authorities decided it would be best to expel Bahá'u'lláh from the country in order to halt the growth of the movement. They believed that if they removed the visible head of the Faith the followers of The Báb would soon disperse. Therefore, He was exiled to Baghdad, Iraq, forcing Him and His family to traverse the Zagros Mountains, on foot and on horseback, in the middle of winter in 1853 with intention that He would perish in such perilous conditions. Despite the hardships, Bahá'u'lláh, his relatives and friends accompanying Him did not perish. The trip lasted from January through April before they arrived at Baghdad.

Bahá'u'lláh lived in Iraq for the next ten years, during which time His leadership of the Bábís grew. His new followers increased in numbers. They came to visit and consult Him, coming even from Iran. The Prime Minister of Iran, not please on how the Faith was growing in Iraq, managed to convince the Ottoman government that ruled Iraq, to exile Bahá'u'lláh once more. This time He was sent to Constantinople (Istanbul today). Before leaving Baghdad, in April of 1863, He had a 12-day farewell meeting with his followers on an island in the Tigris River during which He revealed that He was the Manifestation of God proclaimed by The Báb.

His exile in Constantinople lasted only four months. From there He and His family were again forced to continue the exile to Adrianapole (today known as Edirne), located at the intersection of the Turkish, Greek and Bulgarian borders in Northwest Turkey, where He resided for four years and four months. During this time, He sent personal letters to the kings and rulers of the world announcing that He was God's next Manifestation and requesting them to acknowledge Him as such. It's no coincidence that historians have noted that Mohammed did something similar when, during his seventh year of wandering, He had his emissary, Abdullah Huzafah Sahmi Qarashi, deliver a letter to the king of Sassania, Khusro Perviz, inviting him to join Islam. It is said that when Mohammed learned that Perviz had scornfully torn the letter, He pronounced, "Let his kingdom fall", which did happen at the hands of Byzantine troops who imprisoned and subsequently executed him. (10)

After Adrianople, Bahá'u'lláh was banished even further to the prison-town of Akka, on the Bay of Haifa (located in present day Israel), the furthest point of the Ottoman Empire at the Eastern end of the Mediterranean. He was sent there under the assumption that He would die due to the terrible jail conditions, coupled to the lack of sanitation and presence of mortal diseases. The enormous distance and formidable obstacles did not prevent many of Bahá'u'lláh's followers from making the trip from Iran and Iraq to Akka to visit Bahá'u'lláh in prison and later during His house arrest.

It was during the latter part of His life (in about 1873) that Bahá'u'lláh wrote this most important book of His Revelation, the *Kitáb-i-Aqdas,* known as the *Most Holy Book.* In it are recorded the laws of life given by Bahá'u'lláh to His followers as the most effective means of reaching their ultimate goal, being in the Presence of God. Additionally, He created the outline of what would become the foundation of the Bahá'i Administration and the new world order to come, the arrival of God's Kingdom on Earth. His Writings also included a multitude of letters addressing many diverse topics from spiritual advice to clarifications of the meaning of specific difficult verses of the Qur'an and the Bible, the revelation of multiple prayers for various needs; the exposition of spiritual truths such as the afterlife, the nature of the soul, the equality of man and woman from the moment of their creation and the relationship of God with the soul.

Bahá'u'lláh's earthly life ended on May 29, 1892. He left behind a handwritten Will and Testament naming His oldest son, 'Abdu'l-Bahá, as His successor, the Center of the Covenant, and the sole interpreter of his writings. In turn, 'Abdu'l-Bahá, in his own hand written Will named his grandson, Shoghi Effendi, as his successor and Guardian of the Faith. Because Shoghi Effendi was childless, there was no family successor. Instead of naming a successor, Shoghi Effendi left behind additional guidance for the establishment and functioning of the ruling body of the Bahá'i Faith, the Universal House of Justice, as was outlined by Bahá'u'lláh and expounded by Abdu'l-Bahá. The election of this supreme body took place in 1963.

This governing body consists of nine members elected by each member of the National Spiritual Assemblies (NSA) of the countries where they are present. These National Spiritual Assemblies are conformed by nine members, who are elected by 19 delegates elected by the Baha'is of each country. The NSA members of all the countries where the Faith is present meet in an International Convention every five years in Haifa for the election of the Universal House of Justice and to consult on the Faith's worldwide development. All Bahá'i elections: local, national, and this International Convention are conducted in a prayerful atmosphere, by secret ballot, without nominations or election campaigns for or by any of the Convention participants. The Universal House of Justice is assured of having spiritual assistance in making decisions that will guide the consolidation of its Cause worldwide.

Affirmation of being God's Spokesperson

Bahá'u'lláh repeatedly states that He has come as a representative of God with a Mission to speak in His name. Two quotations from His Writings clearly and assertively affirm this:

> **"When I contemplate, O my God, the relationship that bindeth me to Thee, I am moved to proclaim to all created things 'verily I am God'; and when I consider my own self, lo, I find it coarser than clay!".** (11)

> **"Glory be to Thee, O my God! My face hath been set towards Thy face, and my face is, verily, Thy face, and my call is Thy call, and my Revelation Thy Revelation, and my self is Thy Self, and my Cause Thy Cause, and my behest Thy behest, and my Being Thy Being, and my sovereignty Thy sovereignty, and my glory Thy glory, and my power Thy power."** (12)

Simultaneously He recognizes this is not a choice made by him, but by God:

> **"Thou art He, O my God, Who hath raised me up at Thy behest, and bidden me to occupy Thy seat, and to summon all men to the court of Thy mercy".** (13)

Jesus expressed the same affirmation with equal clarity, "**... the Father who sent Me gave Me a command, what I should say and what I should speak."** (Jn.12, 49) As Jesus declared His obedience to the Will of God so does Bahá'u'lláh reconfirms that this is why He has come:

> **"I have no will but Thy will, O my Lord, and cherish no desire except Thy desire. From my pen floweth only the summons, which Thine own exalted pen hath voiced, and my tongue uttereth naught save what the Most Great Spirit hath itself proclaimed in the kingdom of Thine eternity. I am stirred by nothing else except the winds of Thy will, and breathe no word except the words which, by Thy leave and Thine inspiration, I am led to pronounce".** (14)

> **"It is Thou Who hast commanded me to tell out the things Thou didst destine for them in the Tablet of Thy decree and didst inscribe with the pen of Thy Revelation, and Who hast enjoined on me the duty of kindling the fire of Thy love in the hearts of Thy servants, and of drawing all the peoples of the earth nearer to the habitation of Thy throne".** (15)

The conviction with which Bahá'u'lláh knows Himself to be speaking in God's name, at no time compromises His awareness that He is an insignificant man within whom the Divine Reality inhabits:

> "Say: "Naught is seen in my temple but the Temple of God, and in my beauty but His Beauty, and in my being but His Being, and in myself but Himself, and in my movement but His Movement, and in my acquiescence but His Acquiescence, and in my pen but His Pen, the Precious, the Extolled." (16)

> "When I contemplate, O my God, the relationship that bindeth me to Thee, I am moved to proclaim to all created things "verily I am God"; and when I consider my own self, lo, I find it coarser than clay!" (17)

This is a clear statement of who the Manifestation affirms to be, that he is not God Himself, the Infinite, the Eternal that has incarnated in his humanity. Rather it is the recognition of his humanity made divine by the purity and perfection of the Divine Attributes present in him.

The return of all previous Messengers

We have explained how the Manifestation is like a perfect mirror whose polished surface reflects God's attributes among men because He is like a perfect surface, burnished and unstained, capable of reflecting God's reality to those willing to hear His Revelation. Shoghi Effendi, the great grandson of Bahá'u'lláh, expressed this mysterious reality with these clarifying thoughts:

> "All the Prophets of God, His well-favored, His holy and chosen Messengers are, without exception, the bearers of His names and the embodiments of His attributes... These Tabernacles of Holiness, these primal Mirrors which reflect the Light of unfading glory, are but expressions of Him Who is the Invisible of the Invisibles." (18)

One way of being certain that He who claims to be God's Spokesperson is so, is the degree by which He identifies with the historical Manifestations that preceded him in the same role, that of making God's presence visible to those wishing to listen to Him.

Bahá'u'lláh frequently referred to himself as "the Promised One" that all religions, all cultures and all peoples and ethnic groups on the planet were waiting for at that moment in time. Christians expected the Return of Christ; Buddhists, "the fifth Buddha", some Moslems awaited two Teachers, whom the Bahá'is believe were The Báb and Bahá'u'lláh. The American Indians, Hindu, Zoroastrians, and all peoples on earth expected that a Divine emissary would appear to guide them towards the Golden Age of harmony, unity and peace; and the development for which Jesus prayed, the building of God's Kingdom on Earth.

Bahá'u'lláh clearly and repeatedly stated that these promises, these prophecies, these hopes and expectations referred to Him, to His Message, to His teachings and the community of His united believers because He is the 'Promise of All Ages'. His arrival and appearance fulfills the prophecies and expectations that Humanity had until then. This is how He gives testimony of it:

> **"I bear witness that Thou hast in truth fulfilled Thy pledge and hast made manifest the One (Bahá'u'lláh) Whose advent was foretold by Thy Prophets, Thy chosen ones and by them that serve Thee He hath come from the heaven of glory and power, bearing the banners of Thy signs and the standards of Thy testimonies". (19)**

Let us now examine if Bahá'u'lláh fulfills the criteria of the true Messenger of God.

The "golden measure" of the true Spokesperson of God

The criteria to judge if the one that claims to be speaking in the name of God is authentic or not was given by Jesus, "**... by their fruits you will know them**". (Mt.7:15) When one examines Bahá'u'lláh's life one can find the fruits of the Spirit as the qualities that all sincere seekers perceived when they were in His presence. Which were those fruits of the Spirit? The same as those identified by Paul in his letter to the Galatians, "**But the fruit of the Spirit is love, joy, peace, longsuffering, kindness, goodness, faithfulness, gentleness, self-control**." (Gal.5: 22-23)

Bahá'u'lláh not only renounced the position offered to him as Minister of the King when His father died, but accepted and lived under the consequences when He declared himself a follower of The Báb. His worldly wealth and possessions were taken away from Him. He was placed in a hideous prison, was exiled with his family out of his home country; he and his family had to cross the mountain range in winter with insufficient provisions and adequate clothing. Ten years later He was exiled once more to Constantinople, again having to cross a mountain range, and from there exiled to Adrianapole and finally to the prison-town of Akka near Haifa in modern day Israel. When He died, He left no earthly possession of value other than the treasure of His Revelation and teachings. Completely conscious of his Mission Bahá'u'lláh expressed it in this manner, "**We, verily, have come for your sakes, and have borne the misfortunes of the world for your salvation**." (20)

Every Manifestation has to endure the sufferings inflicted by the enemies that wish to destroy Him, at times making their life unbearable. To avoid such pain the only thing the Manifestation has to do is to renounce to the Mission given to him and to stop offering any more Revelation. At that moment the mistreatments would stop. Bahá'u'lláh, faithful to His Mission, did not hesitate one moment to endure being made a prisoner and to be exiled from His home country until the day He died.

This is how 'Abdu'l-Bahá summarized his father's life's Mission:

"...Bahá'u'lláh, who, during His life, bore innumerable trials and persecutions in order to show forth to the world of mankind the virtues of the World of Divinity, making it possible for you to realize the supremacy of the spirit, and to rejoice in the Justice of God". (21)

What a wonderful way to express a Manifestation's fidelity to His Mission.

Bahá'u'lláh fulfills the prophesies of the second coming

There are many prophecies of the second coming of Jesus. We will present the most salient fulfilled by Bahá'u'lláh. We can start by pointing out the place where the return of the Spirit of Jesus was to establish Himself. Bahá'u'lláh lived His last 25 years in Akka, located on the Bay of Haifa, Israel. Mount Carmel is also found there as is known in the Bible as the Mountain of God. After prison officials relaxed their strict control, Bahá'u'lláh was able to visit Mount Carmel and designated the location where the remains of The Báb were to be interred. Today the Shrine of The Báb rises majestically upon this mountain. The Administrative buildings of the Baha'i Faith were built close to the Shrine. One of them houses the supreme governing body of the Faith, the Universal House of Justice, which directs the followers of Bahá'u'lláh worldwide. This fulfills a prophesy of Isaias, **"The excellence of Carmel and Sharon. They shall see the glory of the LORD, The excellency of our God".** (Isa. 35:1-2) We must remember that the name of Bahá'u'lláh means the *"Glory of God"*.

From where would He come?

There are two prophecies that indicate from where the Spirit of Jesus would return. The first one is from the prophet Micheas, which states that He would come from Assyria and from two fortified cities (Malachi) 7:11. Iraq is situated where Assyria used to be in time of Micheas. The two fortified cities to which the prophet makes reference are Constantinople and Akka, both fortified by a wall that defended them from enemy attacks. The second prophecy stated that He would come from the East (Eze.43:2), which is precisely where Iran and Iraq were found, to the east of Israel. Additionally he was to come from mountain to mountain. In His first exile trip from Iran to Iraq Bahá'u'lláh had to cross the mountain range of Zagros and in His exile trip to Constantinople He had to cross the mountain range to the north of Iraq and Turkey, probably the Taurus mountains as they were called then. The prophecy also said He was to come from sea to sea. Bahá'u'lláh had to travel on ship via the Black Sea, the Aegean Sea and the Mediterranean Sea before arriving as a prisoner at the prison-town of Akka on the bay of Haifa.

How was He to come?

He would come as a thief in the night (2 Pet. 3:10) and unexpectedly (Mat. 24:36). This is how both The Báb and Bahá'u'lláh appeared in Persia. Both came silently as 'a thief in the night', without any great external announcement of their arrival. They took the Persians by surprise even though there had been a great movement of expectation among Islamic scholars for the year 1260. Similarly, Christian Bible scholars had deciphered that the prophesized days of Jesus return was to be in the year 1844. In the US, a national movement led by Rev William Miller, who predicted the year, month and day in which the return of Jesus was to happen. Thousands were ready on the hilltops waiting for Him to descent physically from the heavens. When this did not happen, the movement dissolved, and from it, two Christian denominations were born, the Seventh Day Adventists, and the Jehovah's Witness.

The time of arrival, according to Daniel's prophecy in the Bible, was 1844, the same year in which The Báb announced He was the awaited Qá'im, which meant 'He who will rise' and identified by Shiite Islam as the twelfth Iman who had been in hiding for centuries. The year 1844 is the same year 1260 in the Islamic calendar.

He will come with a new name (Isa. 62:2) and (Rev.2:17). This meant that when Jesus would return He would not have the same name of Jesus. Bahá'u'lláh affirms He is the return of the Spirit of Jesus which refers to His spiritual everlasting reality, not to His physical presence. His new name is Bahá'u'lláh, which in Arabic means "*the Glory of God*".

His return will be accompanied by specific events such as that the Gospel will be preached all over the world. Around the 1840's, Biblical societies had sprung up all over the world, translating the Bible into the main known languages of the time, giving the chance for millions to have access to Jesus' teachings. The Gospel author also pointed out that Jesus would return when there would be wars and rumors of wars (Mt.13: 7-10). It suffices to remember that during Bahá'u'lláh's time, and since, there were several world conflicts, such as the fall of Napoleon III Empire as a result of the Franco-Prussian War, the downfall of the Ottoman Empire, and the fall of the Shah of Persia. All were driven by the spiritual energy unleashed by the coming of the new Christ Spirit.

He will come as the Prince of Peace. The Bahá'i Faith proclaims as one of its tenets the inevitable arrival of World Peace. Bahá'u'lláh's Revelation proclaims this Peace and since He is the Revealer, He also becomes the author of such peace. This is the reason why He earns the title 'Prince of Peace'.

He will carry on His shoulders a new government: this is the proclamation of Bahá'u'lláh's New World Order. Additionally He will sit on the Throne of David (symbolically, He will reign in Israel where David reigned). The visible expression of this prophecy is that the Administrative Center of the Bahá'i Faith, is found on Mount Carmel in Haifa, Israel, Isaiah's Mountain of God.

He will come as the Spirit of Truth, the Comforter, the Counselor: John, the Evangelist, made an allusion to an aspect of Truth when he said that He (Jesus) "**will give witness of me and will glorify me**" (Jn. 15:26, 16:14) This is precisely what Bahá'u'lláh does when He affirms in his Letter to the Christians: "**Say, is this the One** (Bahá'u'lláh) **Who hath glorified the Son** (Jesus**) and hath exalted His Cause**". (22) And in another of his Tablets (letters) Bahá'u'lláh affirmed: "**Oh, followers of the Son... Say, verily, He** (Jesus) **hath testified of Me, and I do testify of Him**". (23)

As to the Comforter, John said: "**However, when He, the Spirit of Truth, has come, He will guide you into all truth**". (Jn. 16:13) and Bahá'u'lláh proclaimed that He was that Spirit of Truth who had come to guide us:

> "**Proclaim then unto all mankind the glad-tidings of this mighty, this glorious Revelation. Verily, He Who is the Spirit of Truth is come to guide you unto all truth. He speaketh not as prompted by His own self, but as bidden by Him Who is the All-Knowing, the All-Wise**". (24)

In another of his letters Bahá'u'lláh shows us how He "**will guide you to the complete truth**" when He explains how we should understand the double language of the sacred scriptures and how that distinction should help us to make the correct interpretation of them:

> "**It is evident unto thee that the Birds of Heaven and Doves of Eternity speak a twofold language. One language, the outward language, is devoid of allusions, is unconcealed and unveiled; that it may be a guiding lamp and a beaconing light whereby wayfarers may attain the heights of holiness, and seekers may advance into the realm of eternal reunion. Such are the**

unveiled traditions and the evident verses already mentioned. The other language is veiled and concealed, so that whatever lieth hidden in the heart of the malevolent may be made manifest and their innermost being be disclosed". (25)

In the "**last days**" and "**the end of times**", the seals of the scriptures shall be opened: At the end of the Prophetic Cycle, Bahá'u'lláh has opened the seals of all the sacred texts and has given us the keys to open those texts. He does this in such a way that it will be possible to establish the unity of the world and the Kingdom of God on Earth. This opening of those seals is found in the last Writings of Bahá'u'lláh where He explains the correct meaning of some key passages of the Gospels and the Koran.

Prophecies of Bahá'u'lláh that have been fulfilled

Unfortunately, the closest followers of the founder of the majority of the religions, once He dies, have fought internally to become the successor of the group. This struggle created internal divisions in many of the world religions, which have resulted in forming different denominations or groups with irreconcilable doctrinal antagonisms. Such is the case in Christianity, which has the Coptic Orthodox Church, the Greek Orthodox Church, the Byzantine Church, the Russian Orthodox Church, the Roman Catholic Church, and the over 10,000 Christian denominations that have sprung forth from the Protestant Reformation. All of them affirm that they are the authentic Christian Church. In Islam, there was a division right after the death of the Prophet. The followers of Ali became known as the Shiites, and the other group known as the Sunnis, and today there are numerous subdivisions within each group based on the different interpretations made of the Koran. The irreconcilable differences are best expressed in the manner in which today Shiites and Sunnis kill each other using suicide bombers. They have killed more people in this manner in Iraq during 2011-12 in an attempt to take control of the government than the number that died during the invasion that overthrew Hussein. (26)

Bahá'u'lláh promised that His Faith will triumph and that His fundamental principle of the unity of religion will prevail. In contrast to other faiths which began to split during their first hundred years the Bahá'í Faith has not been divided in its first 172 years. Attempts made by some of Bahá'u'lláh's relatives to seize control during His life time and soon after his passing have only strengthened the followers of the Founder's wishes of unity of His Cause as expressed in His Will and Covenant. The Faith remains united among its over six million followers in 189 independent countries and 46 dependent territories. Its rich diversity includes people coming from all races, creeds, and cultural backgrounds, including over 2,100 different ethnic groups.

Prophecies made by Bahá'u'lláh that have already been fulfilled are: WW I and WW II, the downfall of Ottoman Empire (27), the downfall of Napoleon III and his empire (28), and the dissolution of the Ottoman Empire (29), the downfall of the Muslim Caliphate (30), the crumbling of the Qajar Persian Dynasty, and the downfall of the Czar of Russia, Alexander II (31). All except Napoleon III had existed for many centuries, but fell within half a century.

Partial Conclusion

We have presented the most important events in the life of The Báb and Bahá'u'lláh which show how both of them fulfilled the criteria that would have to be met by anyone who claimed to be a Messenger, the Mouthpiece of God, so that we could believe in them and the validity of their Revelations.

Although the Báb initiated a new cycle of spiritual evolution for humanity, He announced that the Promised One, Bahá'u'lláh, would appear after him, and that His station would be greater than the His. Bahá'u'lláh did appear as a true Manifestation fulfilling all the criteria that allows us to believe in Him as a

Spokesperson for God. He presented a still broader Revelation as foretold by the Báb. Since Bahá'u'lláh did appear and fulfilled the criteria of a true Messenger of God, the Baha'i Faith affirms that He is the most recent Manifestation to Humanity.

Chapter 8
References

1) Cited by Shoghi Effendi in *The Dawn-Breakers*, p. 106, in a footnote quoting from Esselmont's *Bahá'u'lláh and the New Era,* pg.29-30.

2) Shoghi Effendi, *The World Order of Bahá'u'lláh*, second ed. rev. (Wilmette: Bahá'í Publishing Trust, 1974, p. 62. (Bahá'u'láh, *Tablets of Bahá'u'lláh*, p. 77

3) The Báb. *Selections from the Writings of the Báb*, p. 105.

4) Ibidem, p. 84

5) Bahá'u'lláh, *Tablets of Bahá'u'lláh Revealed after the Kitáb-i-Aqdas* (Wilmette: Bahá'í Publishing Trust, 1995), p. 12. (Bahá'u'lláh, *The Summons of the Lord of Hosts*, p. 62)

6) The Báb, *Selections from the Writings of the Báb*, pg. 26 - p. 10

7) Shoghi Effendi, *God Passes By*, p. 57

8) Bahá'u'lláh,*Tablets of Bahá'u'lláh*, p. 102

9) Nabil's Narrative, *The Dawn-Breakers*, p. 249 - J.E. Esslemont's *Bahá'u'lláh and the New Era*, and is the words of the author recalling what he heard from 'Abdu'l-Bahá

10) http://en.wikipedia.org/wiki/Muslim conquest of Persia*Tabaqat-i Kubra, vol. I, page 360; Tarikh-i Tabari, vol. II, pp. 295, 296; Tarikh-i Kamil, vol. II, page 81 and Biharul Anwar, vol. XX, page 389*

11) Bahá'u'lláh: *The Kitáb-i-Aqdas*: Notas, Pag: 234

12) Bahá'u'lláh: *Prayers and Meditations*, CXLII, p. 230 XLII,

13) Bahá'u'lláh: *Prayers and Meditations*, LXVI, p. 106

14) Bahá'u'lláh: *Prayers and Meditations*, LXVI, p. 107

15) Bahá'u'lláh, *Prayers and Meditations*, LXVI, p. 106

16) Bahá'i books, Dr. J.E. Esslemont, Bahá'u'lláh and the New Era, pg. 46

17) Bahá'u'lláh: *The Kitáb-i-Aqdas*: Pag: 234

18) Shoghi Effendi, *The World Order of Bahá'u'lláh*, p. 113

19) Bahá'u'lláh, *Tablets of Bahá'u'lláh*, p. 115
20) Bahá'u'lláh, *The Proclamation of Bahá'u'lláh*. p. 91
21) Shoghi Effendi, *The World Order of Bahá'u'lláh*, p. 113
22) Abdu'l-Bahá, *Paris Talks, p. 160*
23) Bahá'u'lláh *Tablets of Bahá'u'lláh*, p. 12
24) Bahá'u'lláh, *Tablets of Bahá'u'lláh*, p. 10
25) Bahá'u'lláh, *The Kitab-i-Iqan*, p. 254
26) Google.Casualties Iraq war Database Iraq Body Count https:// www.iraqbodycunte.org/database/ --- Casualties of the Iraq War – Wikipedia, the free encyclopedia en.wikipedia.org/wiki/Casualties_ of_ the_ Iraq_War
27) Shoghi Effendi, *God Passes By*, p. 345
28) Baha'u'llah, *The Proclamation of Baha'u'llah*, p. 20
29) Shoghi Effendi, *God Passes By*, p. 231
30) Baha'u'llah, *The Kitab-i-Aqdas*, p. 217, No. 120
31) Shoghi Effendi, *God Passes By*, p. 227

Chapter 9

The New Revelation

Similar to other Manifestations whose Revelation gave origin to a new religion in the world, The Báb and Bahá'u'lláh affirmed repeatedly God's autonomy as the essential reality of God: there is only one God and there is no other god beside Him. Teaching this essential truth of God was the titanic effort that Abraham and Moses had to make until the end of their lives so that the People of Israel would recognize 'Yahweh' (Hebrew word to refer to the only God) as their only God. Jesus added a new characteristic to the Only God of the Israelites, that of being an ever forgiving, merciful, and loving Father making it possible to have an intimate dialogue with Him. Mohammed emphasized once more that 'there is no other god, but Allah (the Arabic word chosen to refer to God). The Báb and Bahá'u'lláh constantly reminded their followers of God's oneness, His role as the Creator of everything that is, dependent on no one, Self-subsisting. The following quotes will suffice to show how this fundamental truth of God is reiterated repeatedly in their writings as the fundamental truth from which all other affirmations about God emanate.

The Báb

"Verily He is the All-Compelling, the All-Glorious; and no God is there other than Him, the sovereign Ruler, the Almighty...". (1)

"...whereas hadst thou been among such as are endowed with the knowledge of the Bayan, thou wouldst have, at the sight of the Book, testified forthwith that there is no God but Him, the Help in Peril, the Self-Subsisting". (2)

"What is there in the Bayan which keepeth thee back from recognizing these verses as being sent forth by God, the Inaccessible, the Most Exalted, the All-Glorious?" (3)

"Verily, verily, I am God, no God is there but Me; in truth all others except Me are My creatures. Say, O My creatures! Me alone, therefore, should ye fear'. (4)

"GOD testifieth that there is none other God but Him, the Almighty, the Best Beloved". (5)

"HALLOWED be the Lord in Whose hand is the source of dominion. He createth whatsoever He willeth by His Word of command 'Be', and it is. His hath been the power of authority heretofore and it shall remain His hereafter. He maketh victorious whomsoever He pleaseth, through the potency of His behest. He is in truth the Powerful, the Almighty. Unto Him pertaineth all glory and majesty in the kingdoms of Revelation and Creation and whatever lieth between them. Verily He is the Potent, the All-Glorious. From everlasting, He hath been the Source of indomitable strength and shall remain so unto everlasting. He is indeed the Lord of might and power. All the kingdoms of heaven and earth and whatever is between them are God's, and His power is supreme over all things. All the treasures of earth and heaven and everything between them are His, and His protection extendeth over all things. He is the

Creator of the heavens and the earth and whatever lieth between them and He truly is a witness over all things". (6)

Bahá'u'lláh

If The Báb was direct in affirming repeatedly the Oneness of God before Whom there is no other God, Bahá'u'lláh was equally profuse:

"Deprive me not, O my Lord, of the splendors of the light of Thy face, whose brightness hath illuminated the whole world. No God is there beside Thee, the Most Powerful, the All-Glorious, the Ever-Forgiving". (7)

"Thou art, verily, He Whose grace hath guided them aright, He Who hath declared Himself to be the All-Merciful. No God is there but Thee, the All-Glorious, the Supreme Helper". (8)

"No God is there beside Thee, the Mighty, the Ever-Abiding, the All-Bounteous, the Most Generous". (9)

"Thou art, verily, the Almighty, the Most Exalted, the All-Glorious, the Most Great". (10)

"There is none other God but Thee, the Guardian, the Self-Subsisting". (11)

"There is none other God but Thee, the Inaccessible, the Omnipotent, the Omniscient, the Holy of Holies". (12)

"Thou art He who from everlasting hath, through the potency of His will, been all-powerful, and will continue to remain the same forever and ever". (13)

"Glorified be Thy name, O Thou Who art the King of all Kings!" (14)

"Potent art Thou to do as Thou willest. No God is there but Thee, the Almighty, the Most Powerful". (15)

"Praised be Thou, Who art the Lord of all creation". (16)

These quotes gives us the basis for understanding some of the new principles that derive from the Revelation of Bahá'u'lláh that are logical consequences of the Unity, Self-subsisting and Omnipotence of who God is.

Religious persecution and warfare

As we look at historical information and current affairs, we are able to see how religion has been one of the principle motives for multiple violent encounters between tribes, empires, nations. It suffices to remember the bloody conquests carried out by the Israelites on their 'enemies', neighbors or those living in the 'promised land'. Moses assured the Israelites that **'The Lord will fight for you'** before the crossing of the Red Sea (Ex. 14:14). The assistance of God is obvious when the Pharaoh's army is destroyed by the engulfing waters of the Red Sea as commanded by Moses to close upon them (Ex. 14:15-31). Another intervention of God is made evident in the battle between Israel and Amalek (1 Sam. 28:18); in the encounter of David with the Amalekites (1 Sam.30: 1-20); in the battle of Jericho (Jos. 6: 1-16); God is also present in the battle of Joshua against Makkedah, against Libna, Lachish and Horam, and the king of Gezer (Jos. 10: 28-33). The Israelite foes were so beaten that they were deprived from holding their territory as it was consigned in the book of Joshua:

"These *are* the kings of the land whom the children of Israel defeated, and whose land they possessed on the other side of the Jordan toward the rising of the sun, from the River Arnon to Mount Hermon, and all the eastern Jordan plain". (Jos. 12:1). And if this had not been enough the people of God were given the promise that God will give them the territories of the Philistines, Canaanites, and Gebalites along with all of Lebanon (Jos. 13:1-6)

When the first Christians started witnessing their faith in the Resurrected Messiah, the Jewish religious leaders fell upon them because they could not allow an open teaching of such facts, considered to be heresies from the Jewish official doctrine. They started a full scale persecution of Christians. Saul of Tarsus was appointed by the religious rulers to oversee the persecution and was the garment keeper of those that stoned the first Christian martyr, Steven. Saul, on his way to Damascus, to persecute more Christians, had a spiritual revelation from Jesus, powerful enough to convert him into one of his most outspoken followers. As a Christian, he became known as Paul. The Roman Emperors also persecuted the Christians when they proclaimed an allegiance to the Only One God above the Emperor; a belief not tolerated by the 'absolute' monarch of the moment. The captured Christians who refused allegiance to the Emperor above God were sacrificed in the Coliseum to the wild beasts giving the Roman populace an extraordinary testimony of faith they had not witnessed before.

Centuries later Christians started the legendary Crusades against Islam under the slogan 'recovery of the Holy Places is our divine right' since Jesus had lived and preached there. Historical records vary, but from 20,000 - 30,000 Muslims were literally massacred during the first conquest of Jerusalem under the command of Duke Godfrey. There were eight Crusades, beginning in 1095 until 1290. During those 200 years about a million persons were killed according to Wertheim's calculations, or two million according to Charles Mackay (17) or five million according to Alethia; depending on how each one calculated the human sacrifice of these barbaric religious wars. (18)

The paroxysm of the prohibition to interpret Sacred Scripture reached its peak during the 'Holy Inquisition'. This creation of the Catholic Church was aimed at identifying, persecuting, jailing, torturing, judging and executing men and women accused of being 'heretics' because these individuals asked legitimate questions about the reasons for specific dogmas of the Church that seemed to contradict logical and rational thought. Fray Thomas Torquemada (Valladolid 1420 – Avila 1498) was placed at the head of this organization. He organized the Inquisition in Spain with such effectiveness that it became the model for the rest of Europe. The Jewish historian – Graetz - affirmed that during Torquemada's term, about 2,000 Jews were burned at the stake accused of being 'non repentant sinners'. (19) During the Spanish Inquisition (1478-1834) between 3,000-5,000 men and women were executed to maintain 'the purity of dogmatic truth' as interpreted by the Catholic hierarchy of the time and defended fiercely by the priests who ended up being true persecutors of Christians suspected of being 'heretics'. (20)

During the Spanish Conquest of Central and South America, religion served as the moral and divine justification to enslave, and decimate the indigenous populations of the Aztecs, the Mayans, the Quechuas, the Incas, and the Guaranies under the theological assertion that these 'savages' did not know the True God, and therefore it was the obligation of the missionaries to baptize and literally submit them to the Christian religion. In Bolivia, approximately 8 million indigenous people were sacrificed by forcing them to extract silver from the mines of Potosi. No one knows, with sufficient accuracy, how many indigenous persons were sacrificed during the Spanish Conquest. Conservative estimates affirmed that at the start of the Conquest there were about 70-90 million people between the Aztecs, the Mayans and the Incas. At the end of the Conquest, these numbers had been reduced to about 3.5 million, which represents 66.5 to 86.5 million dead indigenous people. (21)

It must be pointed out that a significant number of these perished because of the epidemics introduced by the 'conquistadores' against which the indigenous had not immunity or treatment. Such was the case of the smallpox epidemic that devastated the Aztecs after their first failed Spanish attack in 1520. All throughout the Americas the sicknesses introduced by the first Europeans - (smallpox, chicken pox, measles, syphilis, and typhoid fever) - killed anywhere's between 65% to 85% of the population (depending on the source and manner of calculating the numbers). (22) Independently if they were killed directly by the conquistadores or by their diseases, the religious motivation served them well to subjugate and conquer these indigenous tribes that already lived in the continent as their legitimate inhabitants, centuries before the Conquistadores arrived.

Modern history remembers painfully the Holocaust of World War II when more than 6 million Jews, and other minorities (including Baha'is) were killed following Hitler's orders, and carried out by his spiritual and morally blind military executioners. The backdrop of this abominable order of Hitler was born out of a profound and fanatical aversion to the Jewish people. He personified them as the most anti-Aryan enemies. Thus, he irrationally ordered their elimination because he was convinced that it was required to allow the "resurgence of a new pure Aryan race".

Al-Qaeda, since its beginnings, declared war on the West because it claimed that the West's worldwide immorality and materialism, was infecting and destroying the purity of Islam. Thus, they declared open war on Westerners, who are 'infidels', and represent these anti-values. The movement had a clear intention to obtain political and religious power, as it could be witnessed in an almost daily basis on the news. The attacks have been constant, as can appreciated by the following short list:

-   A highly publicized attack occurred against the US destroyer, the USS, Cole on October 12, 2000, while it was making a routine stop at the port of Aden, Yemen. A small outboard motorboat was driven into the hull of the destroyer by a group of suicide Muslims who exploded themselves, making a 12 by 12 meters hole, killing 17 sailors and wounding 40. (23)
-   Another attack was carried out in July 7, 2005 on the London underground by a local Al-Qaeda cell who exploded a bomb that killed 56 persons and wounded 700 passengers.
-   The most dramatic attack was the one made against the two World Trade Center Towers in New York on

September 11, 2001, when each of two high jacked commercial airplanes were flown into a tower, both the Western symbol of materialistic commerce, while a third one was made to crash into the Pentagon. There was a fourth hijacked plane that was apparently going to be directed to either the Capitol or the White House but the passengers overpowered the hijackers and made it crash in a rural field in Somerset, Pennsylvania. The multi-pronged took the lives of approximately 2,980. This shows how a fanatical religious ideology can convert religion into the motor, justification and the stimulus to carry out the destruction of human lives 'in the name of God'. (24)

Since 2009, religious motivated terrorist activity or a simple desire to obtain political power has taken hold all around the world. Let us remember some of the most salient events: (25)

- August 19, 2009: Various government buildings were destroyed by bombs in Baghdad, Iraq leaving 102 wounded or dead.
- October 25, 2009: Two vehicles loaded with bombs were exploded against government buildings, again in Baghdad, leaving a total of 155 dead.
- October 28, 2009: A terrorist attack exploded bombs in a marketplace of Pakistan, leaving 118 persons dead or wounded.
- December 8, 2009: Five car bombs were detonated in Baghdad leaving 127 dead/wounded.
- December 30, 2009: A suicide attack in Iraq kills eight American civilians who were in a base in Afghanistan, seven of them CIA agents.
- March 29, 2010: In the metro system of Moscow two suicidal Muslim women, from the volatile region of Dagustan, blew themselves up killing 38 persons and wounding more than 70. (26)
- May 10, 2010: Multiple bombs were detonated in Hilla, Basra, al-Suwayra and other cities of Iraq, leaving a total of 102 dead persons. (27)

- January 24, 2011: A terrorist suicide bomber blew himself up in the Domodedov Airport of Moscow killing 36 persons and wounding 180. The attack was attributed to a militant group from the North of the Caucuses under the control of the Cherchen chief, Doku Umarov, who used religious reasons to justify his attack. (28)

After the death of Osama bin Laden by United States Navy SEALs on May 2, 2011, a new more open extreme Islamic group, ISIS, turned into an army continued Al-Qaeda's wave of terrorism with bomb attacks on civilian and military posts covering the whole year of 2015 into a never ending sequence of deaths in Europe, and the Middle East. Violations Documentation Center in Syria (VDC)), a monitoring organization that gathers information from inside the country to maintain a running count of how many people have died in its nearly five-year-old conflict. Using a three-stage documentation process, the VDC has confirmed the deaths of 4,406 people at the hands of ISIS so far. But these are the numbers they could actually keep track. Rough estimates calculated that they only accounted for about 50 % of those killed. ISIS had also taken control of several key cities in Iraq.

These brief, but packed stories of religiously motivated violence, allows us to better understand how religion has been misused in the past, and serves today as the justification for fanatical extremists to declare war, justify political violence, and act on violent populist manifestos, such as the ones proclaimed by ISIS in the Middle East in 2014 -15.

Oneness of religion and of humanity

Even though the Revelation of Bahá'u'lláh is new, it is anchored in the ancient fundamental belief of all religions that God is One. If God is One and He is the source of the Eternal Word that creates, it is logical to conclude that Revelation from God is One, since it comes from the One God, expressed to humans by God's Spokesperson, the Manifestation. Even though many Manifestations have appeared in history, they are mysteriously

One because of their origin as was explained in Chapter 2. The Unity of God is thus continued in His Word. He may speak many times, through the various Manifestations that have appeared and will appear yet in the future, but it will be the same Word in essence and in origin. In 'Abdu'l-Bahá's words:

> "Briefly, the Holy Manifestations have ever been, and ever will be, Luminous Realities; no change or variation takes place in Their essence. Before declaring Their manifestation, They are silent and quiet like a sleeper, and after Their manifestation, They speak and are illuminated, like one who is awake". (29)

Therefore, the Revelation that God makes to man, along mankind's ever evolving history, is One. The book of Revelation is One, but it comes to mankind by chapters that we call Hinduism, Judaism, Zoroastrianism, Christianity, Islam, among others, and now, the Bahá'i Faith. The author of that one Book of Progressive Revelation is One, God Himself, "**He who is the Lord of all religions...**" (30)

The founders of these religions, the Manifestations sent by God, had as their main Mission that of guiding the human race to its spiritual and moral maturity. To accomplish this, they renewed the pact with God to live according to His teachings. These teachings guide us to achieve our goal of spiritual maturity. The Revelations given by the Manifestations became the civilizing force of those people that received it because the particular Revelation given at that time was precisely what Humanity needed at that moment. As Bahá'u'lláh expressed it:

> "The All-Knowing Physician hath His finger on the pulse of mankind. He perceiveth the disease, and prescribeth, in His unerring wisdom, the remedy. Every age hath its own problem, and every soul its particular aspiration". (31)

The same thought was amplified by his son, 'Abdu'l-Bahá:

"One Holy Soul gives life to the world of humanity, changes the aspect of the terrestrial globe, causes intelligence to progress, vivifies souls, lays the basis of a new life, establishes new foundations, organizes the world, brings nations and religions under the shadow of one standard, delivers man from the world of imperfections and vices, and inspires him with the desire and need of natural and acquired perfections. Certainly nothing short of a divine power could accomplish so great a work". (32)

The fact that each Revelation came through a different Manifestation does not mean that each Revelation has a different source of inspiration, thereby entering in conflict with other Revelations. The conflict has appeared when the interpreters of these religions created the tradition, beliefs and/ or dogmas, within the religion, that affirm that their Revelation is the one authentic, true and unique Revelation of God. Bahá'u'lláh explains that all Revelations have come through a different Manifestation. Each one clarifies what has not been understood from the previous Manifestation's teachings. Given the fact that each new Revelation comes from the same God, the same source, it does not compete with the previous Revelation. It arrives to give fulfillment in what was left pending, to clarify what was not understood from the previous Revelations, to change some practical social behaviors, but above all to ratify what had been revealed of Who God is, and presenting a new facet of His unknowable Essence that had not yet been revealed.

Yet, a question lingers, if God is the same source of Revelation, how come there are so many different religions? This is a valid question since there are at least seven major religions covering the majority of the human race (Hinduism. Hinduism, Judaism, Zoroastrism, Buddhism, Christianity, Islam and the most recent, the Baha'i Faith). When one listens to the convinced followers of the previous revelations to the Baha'i Faith, one perceives that each one has apparent 'irreconcilable differences' with one or several of the other religions.

Putting the question in another way, if the source of inspiration is the One God, why are there differences among religions?

These differences appear because as time goes by more and more human 'experts' and 'authentic interpreters' appear giving multiple interpretations of what the Manifestation taught. In addition to this constant factor being present is the fact that the social teachings given by the Manifestations change from age to age according to the needs of those receiving the new Revelation (See Chapter 4). The interpreters are able to do this because they claim for themselves that role; that of being the only ones capable of making authentic interpretations of that Revelation. Multiple interpretations made by these 'professionals of the faith' have allowed for the appearance of such differences among the content of each Revelation. The phenomenon has been so intense during the history of each religion that even within each Revelation there have appeared several who claimed to have the correct interpretation of a particular Sacred Text or a specific passage and depending on their circle of influence, these interpreters have ended up creating their own church or denomination. Thus, it is not surprising to find that Christianity has over 10,000 denominations each one claiming to have a true interpretation of the message of His Holiness Jesus or any of the other books of the Bible. Each claims to interpret correctly the portion of the original texts on which they base their own doctrinal position.

When this occurs, the time is ripe for the appearance of a new Manifestation who brings a new Revelation. The appearance of a new Messenger from God brings on the emergence of a new spiritual spring, a renewal of the original spirit of the previous religion that no longer generates a vigorous spiritual life in many of its followers. This does not rule out the existence of convinced individuals that live intensely their beliefs.

'Abdu'l-Bahá summarized the process when he affirmed that,

"It is, therefore, clear and evident that the Religion of God does not maintain its original principles among the people, but that it has gradually changed and altered until it has been entirely destroyed and annihilated. Because of this the manifestation is renewed, and a new religion established". (33)

It is in this sense that the Baha'i Faith proposes a radical revision of the heritage that teaches children that their religion was the only one, the true religion and the people who did not accept it were to be considered 'infidels', the 'enemy', the 'Anti-Christ', the 'deceiving devil'. Each person who accepts being a follower of Bahá'u'lláh accepts the validity of the previous Manifestations of God as coming from the Kingdom of God, and speaking in the name of God. Each Manifestation is seen as giving a new Revelation with the power and capacity to renew the vigor and freshness lost along the era of the previous one.

The innovative aspect of the Baha'i Faith is that it accepts like brothers each and every person who professes those other religions as a continuous Revelation of God. The duty of each Baha'i is to share with whosoever wishes to hear the glad tidings of Bahá'u'lláh's new Revelation. He does not impose himself by force or by fanatical arguments to demonstrate the truth of Bahá'u'lláh's declarations; he does it by way of reasoning, reflection, and independent search of the truth. The sacred texts of Bahá'u'lláh are sufficiently clear and powerful to illuminate those who approach them with open mind and heart, ready to listen the new Revelation. Since it comes from God, it has the power to transform the human heart.

The exhortation of Bahá'u'lláh in this aspect is clear and without ambiguities. He requests his followers to proceed in this manner:

"To associate with the followers of all religions with fellowship". (34)

And to:

"... consort, with amity and concord and without discrimination, with the adherents of all religions; warns them to guard against fanaticism, sedition, pride, dispute and contention; inculcates upon them immaculate cleanliness, strict truthfulness, spotless chastity, trustworthiness, hospitality, fidelity, courtesy, forbearance, justice and fairness; counsels them to be "even as the fingers of one hand and the limbs of one body"; calls upon them to arise and serve His Cause; and assures them of His undoubted aid". (35)

Only if all cultures and all religions are accepted as valid and authentic, can there be a possibility of creating a movement whose goal is the unity of the human race. This unity is based on the fact that all religions have as their common goal to bring their followers closer to God, to His Kingdom and His Presence for all eternity. If we accept this common goal, it is possible to understand how religions are all One in their essence; that they come from the same origin, God, Who reveals Himself in each religion.

A new teaching of the Revelation of Bahá'u'lláh is that he has decreed that the Baha'i Faith shall not have clergy to dictate the correct interpretation of His writings because He has declared that the human race has achieved the stage of maturity in which each individual is capable of reading and exploring the Revelation of God and is capable of understanding the Sacred Writings and their application in his daily life. This goal is achievable when the seeker additionally prays, reflects, and consults with others on their meaning and relevance. To aid this process, the Baha'i Sacred Writings have been translated into 800 languages. The youthful, vigorous Baha'i worldwide community will stimulate Humanity to consider the vision of a united Mankind as a global family and the Earth as its sole country.

Unity of Humanity

If God is one, if His Revelation is One and therefore religions, in essence, are One since they come from the same God; then it is easy to understand why one of the central principles of Bahá'u'lláh's Revelation is that Humanity is one, because there is only one race, the human race, and the day of its unification as a global society has arrived. Bahá'u'lláh has affirmed that God has set in motion historical forces that are breaking down traditional barriers of race, class, creed and nation, and that in due time, this breakdown will create a new universal civilization. The beginnings of this dynamic are happening now in the inter-ethnic marriages, which were unthinkable not too long ago. The greatest challenge facing the peoples of the Earth is that of accepting that its unity emanates from the fact that we all have the same divine origin and we are all engaged in the process of unification of Humanity.

Another way of expressing the same principle is the proposal of a new definition of race. What we presently call the 'white race', the 'yellow race', the 'black race' is incorrect. On the planet there is only one race, the human race, which includes all the men and women of all the continents; we are the only human race that exists on the planet. The differences of skin color, color of eyes, the texture, and color of the hair are just different gene combinations that have no role in defining us as humans. If we surgically open the bodies of a black person, a white, and an Asiatic person, we find inside the same design of the nervous system; the same vital organs of the heart, the liver, the pancreas, the kidneys, the lungs, the digestive system; the same circulatory system, the same bone structure made up of the cranium, the spinal column, scapula, the ribs, humerus, hip, femur, toe and hand bones. These individuals have the same mental processes, with the capability of logical deductions, memory, imagination, and emotions. Science, when it finished the mapping of the human genome, found that the differences in the nucleotides among humans, regardless of where they live, are not more than 0.01%; which turns out to be 1 per ten thousand nucleotides between any two persons chosen at random. (36)

When one looks at a human being in this fashion, we become aware how vain is the categorization of belonging to a different race. We share the same internal basic organization whether we are black, white, or Asiatic; whether we give ourselves African, Norwegian, Mayan, Indonesian, Latin American, Irish, German, or Arabic last names. These are just human inventions to give individuality to our external differences. What is sad and hurtful is that based on these external differences we have put together a list of categories that end up giving rise to pejorative stereotypes within which we immediately place people when we see them for the first time. These ethnic prejudices, cultural prejudices, and religious prejudices are the ones that have led us to create the category of 'different races' among members of only one race, the human race. The worst aspect is that we have traditionally loaded such categorization with justified hatred, repulsion, and aggression.

It is not possible to think that we can create the unity of mankind when racial prejudices are the norm for classifying each other, for harassing each other. The creation of a collective consciousness that we are one race, the human race that inhabits the only true country, the Earth, is a necessary step in our advance towards the unity of the human race. The integration of different ethnic, religious, social, and economic differences is clearly reflected in the worldwide Baha'i community. The approximately six million Baha'is not only reside in over 189 independent countries and 46 dependent territories, but their rich diversity encompasses people from the major ethnic groups, creeds and cultures of the planet including representatives of over 2,100 ethnic groups. (37)

To be able to achieve this international community it is imperative that it be backed up and validated by a Revelation that gives such a noble idea the vital spiritual force required to bring it about. Only then will it have a profound impact, capable of renewing the collective consciousness of Humanity. This principle must be proposed to the whole world so that the collective consciousness of our global unity can be awaken to the necessary level to become the driving force of the spiritual development of all the members of the human race, especially of those who make decisions based on racial prejudices that affects us all.

Bahá'u'lláh expresses this idea with the usual potency of His words:

> **"He hath proclaimed: It is not for him to pride himself who loveth his own country, but rather for him who loveth the whole world. The earth is but one country, and mankind its citizens".** (38)

Depending on how fast this idea takes hold in the world, so that it becomes a universal heritage-idea of Humanity, is the speed at which we will be able to erase from our vocabulary the terms of 'black race', 'white race', 'brown race' and refer to ourselves simply as the 'human race'. This recognition of unity that does not negate the minor differences, but considers them as the richness of its species expressed in a multitude of skin color variations, eye colors, different body mass some very tall, others short, some fat other skinny, some very hairy others less, some with crisp hair texture, others with very thin and different hair color. When we can celebrate these differences, acknowledge them as the richness of our incredible species, we will have reached one of the goals proposed by Bahá'u'lláh:

> **"The well-being of mankind, its peace and security, are unattainable unless and until its unity is firmly established".** (39)

This is possible to attain because Bahá'u'lláh himself established that Humanity had reached the threshold of its spiritual development required to be able to posses this collective consciousness when he affirmed:

> **"Behold how the generality of mankind hath been endued with the capacity to hearken unto God's most exalted Word -- the Word upon which must depend the gathering together and spiritual resurrection of all men..."** (40)

To be successful in the promotion of world unity, the Baha'i Faith must be firmly united. The unity of the Faith is guaranteed in the Writings of Bahá'u'lláh and 'Abdu'l-Bahá, His son, who provides authoritative guidance. This guidance includes a Covenant in which such Unity is proclaimed as the purpose of the Revelation of Bahá'u'lláh. It is at present carried out by the administrative body governing the affairs of the international Bahá'i community, the Universal House of Justice. These provisions have protected the Bahá'i community from sectarian divisions during its first critical century and half of existence and have given the Faith the ability to adapt to the requirements of a rapidly evolving civilization.

In addition to the Oneness of God and Humanity the new Revelation of Bahá'u'lláh offers the following innovative principles that we are just enumerating now as an invitation to the reader to search and find the spiritual universe embedded in this most recent Divine Revelation:

- The Unity and relative nature of religious truth and the responsibility of each one of us to search independently for truth.
- The elimination of all forms of prejudice
- The assurance that women and men have equality and equal opportunities in all fields
- The elimination of the extremes of poverty and richness
- The availability of universal education for all
- The establishment of a new world federation of nations
- The establishment of a new World Order

- The Advent of World Peace

You can investigate each one of these tenets in the Bahá'i web page www.bahai.org If you wish to read the principal writings of the Bahá'i Faith you can download the free program, Ocean, available in Spanish and English (and other languages). The web address is www.bahai-education.org Our cordial invitation is that you download the program and look in the Index at the numerous books you can read, consult and print desired quotes on line. They will give you an ample historical vision of the birth of the Faith, an overview of the principal Writings of Bahá'u'lláh, of His son, Abdu'l-Bahá, and of his grandson, the Guardian of the Faith, Shoghi Effendi. There is also the Bahá'í Reference Library, http://www.bahai.org/library which has ample number of books that can be downloaded in pdf or Word versions from that site, or in various eBook formats from www.bahaibookstore.com,

Conclusion

God has spoken to us since we appeared on Earth as it was symbolically expressed in the first book of the Judeo-Christian Bible. He has never stopped talking to us. He has continued to do it throughout history of Humanity using our most natural way of communication among ourselves, the spoken word. It is in the use of the word that we codify our thoughts and confess our fears, our hopes, our sadness, our desires, our questions, our aspirations, feelings and emotions, our beliefs and convictions, our judgments, our condemnations, our forgiveness and our love.

God, who made us 'in His image and likeness', has chosen His Creative Word to communicate with us because the spoken word is the most natural way we humans have to communicate among ourselves. In this manner, God has used our way of communication to make Himself 'one of us'. He has accomplished this by the Manifestation who presents himself as His Spokesperson, becoming His voice and visible presence among men.

Clothed in human form, as a person with whom we could relate, with whom we could communicate and understand His Message because He spoke the language we spoke, God has established a dialogue with mankind that was initiated when we appeared on the planet as humans, and will continue as long as the human race continues in existence. The dialogue is through the Manifestations that are Beings who mirror God in the most perfect way. This is the particular way that God has chosen to be present among men, conversing with us, letting us know the intimacy of His Being, which we are not capable of comprehending by our limited knowledge. The dialogue that God initiated with humanity through the Manifestations has turned into a cascade of uninterrupted Revelation that has nourished us until today with '**spiritual words that give us eternal life**'. Those Luminaries of Being, the Manifestations, have revealed to us aspects of the essence of God to which we had no access. What humans have affirmed in the past and at the present is God's essence has been more the product of their creative mind [4], as compared to what the Manifestations have revealed to us as being God's innermost reality.

When God established this permanent dialogue with us, He pledged to always be with us and to be Faithful to what was promised in the Revelations consigned in the Holy Scriptures of all religions. In those Books, the Word of God has remained with the capacity and force to transform the human heart when it comes in contact with it. This is the mode of communication that God has created and it has always been open, with free access, only limited by the desire and effort of those wishing to come in contact with it.

These monumental Revelations have come down to us adapted to our limited spiritual and intellectual capacity that we had at the moment of their appearance. This is the reason why it has been a Progressive Revelation because Humanity was not prepared to hear the spiritual truths that we have been hearing as each Revelation progressed over time. One excellent example is the new divine prohibition of slavery. During the time of Moses and Jesus, slavery was considered to be the most natural way

---

[4] An excellent example of the creative mind of man to conceive God in 'his own image' is the 1996 book by Franco Ferruchi, *The Life of God (as told by Himself)*, which depicts God as having the same human emotions of fear, confusion, forgetfulness, doubts, disappointment, bewilderment and even sex drive. It is the perfect image of a god that is as frail as any human can be.

of relating to those conquered during battle. Men and women were indisputably considered spoils of war, ant the conqueror was allowed to take them as slaves for all sorts of menial work, for construction of roads and buildings, for mining, for agriculture, for household work.

None of the previous Manifestations prohibited slavery until the appearance of Bahá'u'lláh. Humanity's development was such that even if any of those previous Manifestations had expressed it was God's Will that slavery should be stopped, it was not possible for mankind to hear that message, accept it, much less put it into practice because slavery was the backbone of the economic development in many countries of the world. The ruling class and the beneficiaries of the system were not willing to give up their slaves. The conditions were so compelling that slavery was for a long time not even considered to be morally wrong.

The progressive manner with which God has given us His Revelation is due to our slow spiritual evolution and has been given to us in an appropriate measure for our human capacity to assimilate. It is also the reason why each new Revelation has validated the spiritual essence of the previous one giving the true meaning of the Sacred Texts. Meaning which was hidden in symbolisms, prophecies, and parables. In this sense Revelation is Progressive, because each Manifestation builds on what was revealed by His predecessors, and the most recent one will be relative to the future one to appear (according to Bahá'u'lláh in no less than one thousand years after Him). This relativity of the Revelation is what allows us to grow collectively as much as it demands abandoning firmly established beliefs in order to be able to assimilate the new revealed truths.

With this perspective, one can understand how God's overall Revelation with Humanity is one, since it comes from One God, who is its source. Each Revelation has been the foundation of a movement with a massive cohort of followers. The leaders have structured the content of the Revelation into a religion; the most well known today are Hinduism, Judaism, Buddhism,

Christianity, Islam, and the most recent, the Baha'i Faith; each having its internal organization, its hierarchy, institutions, buildings, jobs, and economic and administrative systems. These structures have, in turn, originated the differences that these religions seem to have. Yet, there is an internal unity since each Founder came from the one and only God. This is why the Bahá'i Faith affirms that all religions are one, since they come from the same Source, God. That they have differences in the way they are lived on a daily basis does not deny or annuls the unity they have in defining God as the One above whom there is no other God. This Unity of God is the fountain of all that can be said about Him and His relationship with us.

We have followed these Revelations throughout history and we have affirmed that there has been a recent Revelation brought to Humanity by two Manifestations of God that appeared in 1844 with The Báb's declaration that He was the return of the long awaited Qá'im of Shiite Islam, and then in 1863, with the declaration of Bahá'u'lláh that He was the Promised one of all the religions, and the Inaugurator of a new cycle of spiritual growth for all Humanity, that of recognizing the Unity of Mankind, the world wide recognition that we all come from the same Creator, and the Advent of World Peace. Bahá'u'lláh has laid out the blueprint for that new world order to come into existence and invites all to participate in the construction of that future, making it possible to experience God's Kingdom on Earth.

The invitation has been made. The reader has two options. The first one is to cast out all that we have expounded as untruthful, impossible to accept because it implies a profound revision of what he/she believed until this moment. The second option is to recognize the logic of what has been elaborated as a simpler, more acceptable way of understanding how God communicates with us continuously throughout mankind's history. God has done it through His Mouthpiece, His messenger, His Manifestation. Any other form of understanding God is inaccessible to our limited capacity of comprehension that cannot know directly the fathomless depth of the Reality of God. We are only able to know His Attributes. Therefore, we need for Him to maintain that continuous dialogue with us, in a way that we can understand Him, and this happens through the Word of the Manifestation.

No one is asked to accept what has been presented in this book without undertaking his/her own investigation. The Sacred Texts of the most recent Revelation of God are available for all those that wish to open their hearts and dive into the ocean of this most august Revelation. Yet, no one can appreciate nor accept its content unless each one takes the plunge. Without fear, without prejudices, without pre-conceptions, the reader is invited to discover in this formidable new Revelation the most surprising answers to today's troubled world questions.

The invitation becomes more powerful with Bahá'u'lláh's own words, which gives us the trust that we need to accept God's invitation:

> **"O SON OF BEING!**
> **With the hands of power I made thee and with the fingers of strength I created thee; and within thee have I placed the essence of My light. Be thou content with it and seek naught else, for My work is perfect and My command is binding. Question it not, nor have a doubt thereof".** (41)

> **"O SON OF BEAUTY!**
> **"By My spirit and by My favor! By My mercy and by My beauty! All that I have revealed unto thee with the tongue of power, and have written for thee with the pen of might, hath been in accordance with thy capacity and understanding, not with My state and the melody of My voice".** (42)

Chapter 9
References

1) The Báb, *Selections from the Writings of The Báb*, p. 20
2) The Báb, *Selections from the Writings of The Báb*, p. 29
3) The Báb, *Selections from the Writings of The Báb*, p. 31
4) The Báb, *Selections from the Writings of The Báb*, VIII, 1p. 97
5) The Báb, *Selections from the Writings of The Báb*, p. 163
6) The Báb, *Selections from the Writings of The Báb*, p. 169
7) Bahá'u'lláh, *Prayers and Meditations*, III, pg. 5
8) Bahá'u'lláh, *Prayers and Meditations*, VI, pg. 9
9) Bahá'u'lláh, *Prayers and Meditations*, X, pg. 13
10) Bahá'u'lláh, *Prayers and Meditations*, XIII, pg. 16
11) Bahá'u'lláh, *Prayers and Meditations*, XVII, pg. 20
12) Bahá'u'lláh, *Gleanings from the Writings of Baha'u'llah*, p. 5
13) Bahá'u'lláh, *Prayers and Meditations*, XXIV, pg. 28
14) Bahá'u'lláh, *Prayers and Meditations*, XXVI, pg 30
15) Bahá'u'lláh, *Prayers and Meditations*, XXX, pg. 34
16) Bahá'u'lláh, *Prayers and Meditations*, XXXIII, pg.43
17) Wertham: 1,000,000. Charles Mackay, *Memoirs of Extraordinary Popular Delusions and the Madness of Crowds*
18) Google: deaths during Crusades) [http://www.bootlegbooks.com/NonFiction/Mackay/PopDelusions/chap09.html]. Aletheia, *The Rationalist's Manual*: 5,000,000. In Twentieth Century Atlas - Historical Body Count (Selected Death Tolls for Wars…
19) "History of the Jews", Philadelphia, 1897, IV, 35 - Tomás de Torquemada
20) Google: Inquisition – Wikipedia enciclopedia
21) Galeano, Eduardo. Las Venas Abiertas de América Latina. Editorial Siglo XXI. Argentina, 1974. pg. 58
22) Google. Epidemias y Conquista Española en América. Catástrofe demográfica en América tras la llegada de los

europeos • La disminución demográfica *es.wikipedia. org/wiki/Conquistadores_españoles*

23) Google: US ship attacked, USS Cole bombing - Wikipedia, the free encyclopedia

24) Google: 9/11: Sept. 11, 2001 attacks, Wikipedia, the free encyclopedia

25) Google. Recent terrorists attacks Map of worst *terrorist attacks* worldwide: 100 or more fatalities www. johnstonsarchive.net/terrorism/globalterrorism1.html

26) Google. BBC News March 29, 2010

27) Google. Worldwide terrorist attacks. Map of worst *terrorist attacks* worldwide: 100 or more fatalities www. johnstonsarchive.net/terrorism/globalterrorism1.html

28) Google. Domodedovo airport attack BBC News - Moscow bombing: Carnage at Russia's *Domodedovo airport*

29) 'Abdu'l-Bahá, *Some Answered Questions*, p. 84

30) Bahá'u'lláh, *The Kitáb-i-Aqdas*, p. 32

31) Bahá'u'lláh, *Gleanings from the Writings of Baha'u'llah*, CVI, p. 212

32) 'Abdu'l-Bahá, *Some Answered Questions*, p. 8

33) 'Abdu'l-Bahá, *Some Answered Questions*, p. 165

34) Bahá'u'lláh, *The Kitáb-i-Aqdas*, p. 159

35) Bahá'u'lláh, *The Kitáb-i-Aqdas*, Preface, p. 14

36) Google. genetic differences between human races. *Race* and *genetics* - Wikipedia, the free encyclopedia *en.wikipedia.org/wiki/Race_and_genetics* –

37) website, bahai.org

38) Bahá'u'lláh, *Gleanings from the Writings of Bahá'u'lláh*, CXVII p. 250

39) Bahá'u'lláh, *Gleanings from the Writings of Bahá'u'lláh*, CXXXI, p. 286

40) Bahá'u'lláh, *Gleanings from the Writings of Bahá'u'lláh*, XLIII p. 96

41) Bahá'u'lláh, *The Arabic Hidden Words*, 12

42) Bahá'u'lláh, *The Arabic Hidden Words*, 67

Bibliography

The majority of the Bahá'i books used for the quotes were found in their corresponding version in the Bahá'i program, 'Ocean" that can be found in the internet ((http:// www.bahai-education.org) as was explained at the end of Chapter 3. The bible quotes are from the Jerusalem Bible and New King James Bible found also in Internet.

'Abdu'l-Bahá, *La Sabiduría de Abdu'l-Bahá*. Conferencias de Paris. 1911. Editorial Bahá'i, Barcelona, España, 1996.

'Abdu'l-Bahá. *Contestación a algunas Preguntas*. Editorial Bahá'i Indolatinoamericana, Buenos Aires, 1994.

'Abdu'l-Bahá. *Promulgación de la Paz Universal*. Editorial Bahá'i Indolatinoamericana, Buenos Aires, 1991.

Armstrong, Karen. *Muhammad, A Bibliography of the Prophet*. Harper, San Francisco, 1993.

Armstrong, Karen. *Islam, A Short History*. Modern Library Chronicles Book. New York, 2000.

Bahá'u'lláh, El Kitáb-I-Iqán, *El Libro de la Certeza*. Editorial Bahá'i de España, Barcelona, 1195

Bahá'u'lláh, Epístola al Hijo del Lobo Título original en inglés: Epistle to the Son of the Wolf. (Ocean Program)

Bahá'u'lláh, La Proclamación de Bahá'u'lláh (Proclamación a los reyes del mundo). Recopilado por la Casa Universal de Justicia. (Ocean)

Bahá'u'lláh, *La Proclamación de Bahá'u'lláh.* Bahá'í World Centre. 1967 by the Universal House of Justice

Bahá'u'lláh, *La Tabla a los Cristianos. AWH-I-AQDAS, La Tabla Más Sagrada.* (Ocean)

Bahá'u'lláh: *Oraciones y Meditaciones.* Traducción del original persa y árabe al inglés por Shoghi Effendi Título original en inglés: Prayers and Meditations by Bahá'u'lláh. (Ocean)

Bahá'u'lláh. *Palabras Ocultas.* Título del original en inglés:*The Hidden Words.* (Ocean)

Bahá'u'lláh, *Pasajes de los Escritos de Bahá'u'lláh.* Spanish version based on the authorized translation in Eglish by Shoghi Effendi, *Gleanings from the Writings of Bahá'u'lláh.* (Ocean)

Bahá'u'lláh, *Tablas de Bahá'u'lláh* Reveladas después del Kitáb-i-Aqdas, Bahá'í World Centre. Haifa (Ocean)

Bahá'u'lláh: *Tablas de Bahá'u'lláh,* Esplendores. (Ocean)

Bahá'u'lláh: *The Kitáb-i-Aqdas.* Bahá'í World Centre. Haifa. 1992 by the Universal House of Justice.

Biblia de Jerusalén. Desclée de Brouwer, Bruxelles, Bilbao, 1967

Campbell, Joseph. *Transformations of Myth Through Time.* Harper Perennial, 1999, reissue.

Cleary, Thomas (translator) *The Essential Koran.* HarperCollins Publishers, 1993.

Effendi, Shoghi. *The World Order of Bahá'u'lláh*, segunda ed. rev. Wilmette: Bahá'í Publishing Trust, 1974.

El Báb. *Selección de los Escritos del Báb*. Romanya Valls, S.A. España, Segunda impresión, 2000.

Esslemont, J.E. *Bahá'u'lláh and the New Era. An introduction to the Bahá'i Faith.* (Ocean)

Ferruchi, Franco, *The Life of God (as told by Himself)*, translation by Raymond Rosenthal, The University of Chicago Press, 1996.

Grun, Bernard. *The Time Tables of History.* Simon & Schuster. Third Revised Edition. New York, 1991.

Marqués, José Luis. *Educadores de la Humanidad. Siete Manifestaciones de un Mismo Dios.* Editorial Bahá'i de España. 2009.

McKenzie, John, S.J. Dictionary of the Bible. The MacMillan Co., N. Y., 1965.

Pareja, Reynaldo, *Sisyphus, the Evolutionary Infancy of Humanity.* Xlibris.com, 2010

Philip, Neil. *Book of Myths, Tales and Legends of the World.* DK Publishing Book. Artes Graficas, Toledo, 1997.

Nabil's Narrative *The Dawn-Breakers.* Translated and Edited by Shoghi Effendi, Bahá'í Publishing Trust, Wilmette, Illinois, 1996.

The Koran. Penguin Classic. Nicolls & Co. Ltd. 1979.

The Teaching of Buddha. Kosaido Printing Co., Tokyo, Japan, 1993.

Edwards Brothers Malloy
Thorofare, NJ USA
March 11, 2016